THE WONDER BOOK OF
HOW IT'S DONE

THE
WONDER BOOK SERIES

ANIMALS *Wild life in Britain* ◆ *African animals* ◆ *wonderland of birds* ◆ *ants and bees* ◆ *world of fishes* ◆ *animals of the past* ◆ *butterflies, moths* ◆ *serpent world, etc.*

RAILWAYS *How a locomotive works* ◆ *famous expresses* ◆ *signals and signalling* ◆ *mountain railways* ◆ *diesel and electric trains* ◆ *railway stations* ◆ *bridges, etc.*

SHIPS *Building a ship* ◆ *ships' officers* ◆ *how charts are made* ◆ *signals and signalling* ◆ *life on an ocean liner* ◆ *yachts and yachting* ◆ *the making of a sailor.*

THE ARMY *Colours and standards* ◆ *Royal Armoured Corps* ◆ *airborne forces* ◆ *traditions* ◆ *armies of the Commonwealth* ◆ *women's service* ◆ *famous soldiers, etc.*

THE NAVY *Ships of the fleet* ◆ *naval guns at work* ◆ *submarines* ◆ *Fleet Air Arm* ◆ *torpedoes and mines* ◆ *naval ways and customs* ◆ *how a warship is navigated, etc.*

AIRCRAFT *Designing and making aircraft* ◆ *piston and jet engines* ◆ *helicopters* ◆ *jet airliners* ◆ *airports* ◆ *aviation as a career* ◆ *airliners past and present, etc.*

WHY & WHAT? *The sun* ◆ *a gramophone* ◆ *coal* ◆ *tea* ◆ *nylon* ◆ *chocolate* ◆ *the moon* ◆ *the stars* ◆ *wool* ◆ *cars* ◆ *water* ◆ *caves* ◆ *volcanoes* ◆ *comets* ◆ *pond life* ◆ *oil, etc.*

WONDERS *Living dragons* ◆ *x-rays* ◆ *ancient Greece* ◆ *tornadoes* ◆ *radium* ◆ *strange and fantastic insects* ◆ *bird plumage* ◆ *the telephone* ◆ *weather balloons, etc.*

NATURE *Birds of the countryside* ◆ *snakes* ◆ *spotting trees* ◆ *birds' nests* ◆ *cleverness of insects* ◆ *king of grasses* ◆ *the seashore* ◆ *tadpoles* ◆ *ants and termites, etc.*

MOTORS *Fast motor cars* ◆ *how a motor car works* ◆ *how to drive* ◆ *traffic lights* ◆ *design and construction* ◆ *commercial vehicles* ◆ *motor cycles* ◆ *motor racing, etc.*

SCIENCE *Our universe* ◆ *molecules and atoms* ◆ *electricity and magnetism* ◆ *light and sound* ◆ *Harwell, atom factory* ◆ *space flight* ◆ *plastics* ◆ *sound barrier* ◆ *3-D, etc.*

DO YOU KNOW? *Tides* ◆ *Severn Bore* ◆ *eclipse* ◆ *Milky Way* ◆ *rainbows* ◆ *radar* ◆ *fog* ◆ *compass* ◆ *colour* ◆ *quicksands* ◆ *coral islands* ◆ *ways of animals.*

TELL ME WHY? *Earthquakes* ◆ *icebergs* ◆ *trade winds* ◆ *oak apples* ◆ *coffee* ◆ *heavy water* ◆ *electro-plating* ◆ *invisible rays* ◆ *canned peas* ◆ *Great Barrier Reef, etc.*

HOW IT'S DONE *Explains what things are and how they are made: golf balls* ◆ *films* ◆ *jewels* ◆ *photographs* ◆ *maps* ◆ *money* ◆ *stainless steel* ◆ *coal* ◆ *radio, etc.*

WOULD YOU BELIEVE IT? *Strange houses* ◆ *insect radio* ◆ *rivers of logs* ◆ *curious plants* ◆ *living giants* ◆ *strange ants* ◆ *fishes of the deep* ◆ *man-made plants, etc.*

THINGS TO DO *Model making* ◆ *camping and hiking* ◆ *indoor games* ◆ *magic* ◆ *stamp collecting* ◆ *match-stick games* ◆ *rowing* ◆ *round games* ◆ *swimming* ◆ *games.*

THE R.A.F. *Famous fighting planes* ◆ *jet fighters and bombers* ◆ *winning your wings* ◆ *men of the aircrew* ◆ *navigation* ◆ *radar* ◆ *bombing up* ◆ *R.A.F. at war, etc.*

THE FARM *Farming through the ages* ◆ *how to be a farmer* ◆ *bacon and eggs* ◆ *tractors and other machinery* ◆ *cattle and other animals* ◆ *corn crops* ◆ *hill farming, etc.*

BIBLE STORIES *Stories from the Old and New Testaments retold in a way that will appeal to children of all ages. Containing 33 fine colour plates by Henry Coller.*

THE STORY WONDER BOOK *A host of delightful stories and poems, and all illustrated with charming drawings in two colours. A book that all ages will enjoy.*

Made IN ENGLAND
Printed in Great Britain by The Whitefriars Press Ltd., London and Tonbridge.

THE
WONDER BOOK
OF
HOW IT'S DONE

WITH SEVEN COLOUR PLATES AND
TWO HUNDRED AND FIFTY ILLUSTRATIONS

Seventh Edition

WARD, LOCK & CO., LIMITED
LONDON, MELBOURNE AND CAPE TOWN

By courtesy of]   [*Dunlop Rubber Co , Ltd.*

TESTING A NEWLY-MANUFACTURED MOTOR TYRE.

In this machine the tyre is rotated at a speed of about 25 m.p.h. by the steel drum. The load is greater than a normal service load and the tyre is run day and night.

Cutting bars of steel into shorter lengths with oxy-acetylene blow torches.

COLOUR PLATES

A B.O.A.C. Constellation airliner having a complete overhaul.

CONTENTS

CONTENTS

By courtesy of]   [Tomson and Wotton Ltd. & Sunbeam Photo Ltd.

Adjusting the temperature of a milk storage tank.

CONTENTS

A potter, whose hands are his tools, shaping a vase that is spinning round before him.

"Subs" at work in the editorial department.

HOW YOUR MORNING NEWSPAPER COMES TO YOU

WHENEVER you are privileged to be present at some important event—the launch of an ocean liner, perhaps, or the opening of a new hospital—you see the newspaper reporters taking down the speeches in shorthand and writing a description of the proceedings in their notebooks. Very soon they will be hurrying back to their offices with their " copy " as they call it, so that you can read the full story at breakfast-time next morning.

When the reporter has typed out his copy from his notes, he takes the manuscript into a big room chiefly furnished with long tables round which the sub-editors sit considering all the piles of contributions for inclusion in the paper. There are hundreds of items—cables from all over the world, letters about happenings in foreign capitals, weather notes from the Air Ministry, stock and share prices from the City, reports from courts of law and football fields and the Houses of Parliament.

Under the window stand several tall wooden boxes with metal

cylinders on the top, out of which thin strips of paper are steadily emitted. These are the "ticker-tapes," news agency telegraph machines automatically sending in still more news details for use in the busy office.

As the sub-editors deal with each piece of copy it is shot off down a long tube to the composing room. Here an operator "taps" it out on the keyboard of a linotype machine, which looks rather like an "outsize" typewriter. On depressing a lettered key a corresponding matrix is released from a magazine and runs down a channel to the assembly box. When a line of matrices is completed, and the necessary spaces inserted, molten metal is pumped into the recessed characters of the matrices, and a solid line of type is produced and ejected on to a metal tray, called a "galley." When the matter is completed, it is transferred to another "galley" and proofs of the matter are taken on a proofing-press. The first proof taken is sent, together with copy, to the Reading Department,

[*Daily Express.*

Compositors making up a newspaper page.

Linotype operators at work in the composing room of " The Times."

where the proof is carefully scrutinised to make sure it conforms exactly with the copy ; in addition, all errors made by the operator are marked for correction.

Bearing a number corresponding to its galley, another proof goes back up the pneumatic tube again. The chief sub-editor approves it and then uses it in making-up the newspaper. He takes the necessary number of sheets, calculates just how much space each proof will require and then marks his sheets with numbers tallying with those on the proofs so that the printers will see just what is to go in and where.

The chief sub-editor must also remember to allot space for the advertisements and the photographic illustrations. These pictures have been collected by the art-editor and are now having process-blocks made from them ready for insertion. Some of the photographs may have arrived by telegraph, employing a wonderful machine with a selenium cell. Selenium is a material particularly susceptible to light and shade, and translates the black and white

["*The Times*".

A battery of presses in the stereotyping foundry.

of the photograph into fluctuating electrical impulses. These impulses cause a stylo travelling over a drum covered with sensitized paper at the receiving end to reproduce faithfully the lights and shades of the original photograph.

As fast as the sub-editor returns his proofs down that ever-busy tube, the galley-columns are arranged to match and transferred one by one to a large metal-topped table until a whole page is complete. Then a metal frame is placed round the type, and to keep it firmly locked together, what is known as " furniture," metal wedges of the same height as the type, are tightened up at the side and bottom. It is then ready for the first stage of its journey towards the printing press.

To meet the requirements of modern rotary printing-machines a semi-cylindrical metal plate must be made from the existing composite pages of type. Sliding into a lift, the page of type is therefore conveyed to the stereotyping foundry, where a mould is obtained by exerting great pressure on a sheet of papier maché material placed in contact with the face of the type. Into this mould molten metal is poured and by the use of a multiplate machine, several semi-cylindrical casts can be quickly obtained. They are then sent on to the printing-room proper to be clamped into place on the gigantic presses.

These are built up on the deck principle, so that the paper travels between several cylinders before emerging as a continuously-printed strip of pages. One touch of a button suffices to set the presses in motion and when you hear their powerful throbbing and see how they shake the foundations, you realise why the printing-room is set in the basement of the newspaper building.

As the presses pour out the printed paper, it passes to a large tray fitted with a descending blade that comes down to meet it and cut it into individual sheets as it emerges. Then these sheets are guided along into an ingenious machine which automatically puts them in proper order and folds them firmly down the middle so that they make the handy-sized newspapers you receive.

Many times during the night the printing presses are stopped

[*The Times*.

Making " blocks " in the process department.

and started and then presently stopped again. The number of copies produced in each period the presses are running is called an edition and has its special name according to the market for which it is intended. For instance, the first edition is naturally those papers which have to be sent some distance by train or lorry so as to arrive next morning. It will leave the presses soon after midnight and will be called the provincial or out-of-town edition. The final edition, often described as the " late local," may only be printed a brief hour or two before you receive it, since the delivery men can collect these papers at the office and carry them in bags to the newsagents' shops, from whence the boy brings your copy to your door by hand.

" News " goes on happening all through the night, so every edition of the paper is different from the rest. Perhaps at one o'clock the telephone will ring frantically to announce that a great fire is raging in the suburbs, and promptly the editor will send a reporter hastening to the scene in a fast car. As there will not be sufficient time for him to come back and type out his copy himself,

Making up in the composing department of " The Times."

Setting up the lines of type.

[*Daily Express.*

he telephones the story of the outbreak from the actual spot and an expert receiver sitting in a sound-proof booth in the newspaper office writes it down on small sheets of paper and hands it to the sub-editors.

One of the pages of type is then quickly recalled from the foundry, two or three columns of less important matter are scrapped and the news of the fire that will take its place is carefully reckoned out so that it fills exactly the same amount of space. Now you see the reason for those little sheets of manuscript. As the sub-editors calculate each one, it can be shot down the tube for the linotype operators to be handling—every minute counts now, for the next edition of the newspaper has to be ready printed at a fixed time so that it can be sent off to the trains and the delivery vans.

In the composing-room the foreman gives each little sheet to one of his operators, who work swiftly together setting up the lines of type. The foreman collects the galley and hurries it off to have a proof " pulled " on the press. This is passed by a sub-editor waiting on the spot and then the galley is placed into its position in the page-case and a new stereo is cast ready for the presses.

This kind of thing takes place several times during the night. At two o'clock may come the tidings of severe floods on the Continent, while twenty minutes later a radio message arrives from Australia with details of an important political Bill that has just been passed. Before the sub-editors have finished dealing with those matters, the newspaper's resident representative in a distant city telephones to say that a famous athlete lies seriously injured there.

Yet so skilful and speedy is the organization of the office, that all the alterations and adjustments are made and the news gets into its proper place in the paper with seldom any hitch. When some outstanding item of copy arrives after the final page-casts are actually being fixed on the presses and it is too late to recall them, then the chief sub-editor puts this news in that little square on one of the pages which is always left vacant for emergency and headed "Stop Press."

The brief sentences are set up in type by hand into a square metal box which is inserted in a special attachment on the press. Naturally, this print is not so clear as the rest, but still you can read it and the news is there.

Out the newspapers pour at precisely the appointed time. They travel along metal tables to be bundled up in quires, each wrapped in several sheets of waste newsprint for protection. Quickly each bundle is corded and labelled with the name of the news-agent for whom it is destined, then off it goes, by train or motor-van or aeroplane, or merely in a delivery man's bag, speeding on its way to your home at breakfast time.

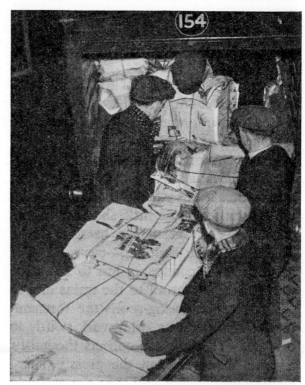

[*Daily Express.*

Loading up a delivery van.

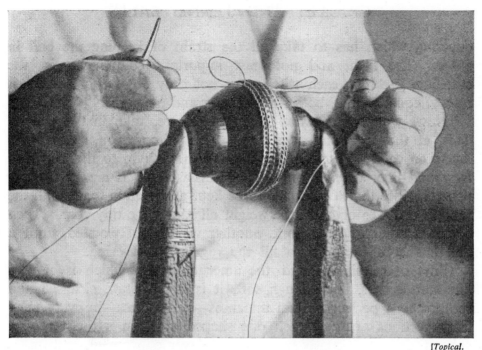

This workman is adding the two outer rows of stitches to a cricket ball.

HOW CRICKET AND TENNIS BALLS ARE MADE

THE cricket ball looks a very simple thing, just a sphere of leather with a few rows of stitching, but in reality it is far from simple. By the laws of the game, a match ball must be not less than nine and not more than nine-and-a-quarter inches in circumference, and not less than five-and-a-half nor more than five-and-three-quarter ounces in weight. The problem confronting the maker is that of building up, within these limits, a ball which will stand the terrific thwack against the bat that scores a " boundary," and at the same time retain its shape. There is yet another problem—that of centring the weight so that there shall be no " bias " in the ball, for, if a bowler is to get accurate spin, the weight of every part of the ball must be exactly equal to its opposite part. To put this more simply : if a cricket ball is cut into any number of equal parts, each part must be of the same weight.

There are no less than five component parts in a match ball : first, the core, then the " quilting," as it is termed, then an inner covering of fine soft leather, and outside that the strong leather covering which has to take all the strain of keeping the ball in shape. The fifth, and not least important component, is the stitching, in which each stitch must not only be of equal size, but also of equal weight, both for the inner and outer rows of stitching.

Now, working outward from the centre, take first the core. This, at the beginning, is a tiny sphere of cork, or a cube with layers on each side to build it into a sphere. On to this tiny ball is wound fine, strong worsted, and this winding is a very delicate process, since the worsted has to be kept at a certain tension all the time in order to equalize the weight all round the tiny core. Then comes another layer of cork, another winding of worsted, until a ball has been built up to fill the regulation covering.

First over this is fitted the inner covering, which is of very fine soft leather, and though soft, it is strong stuff, cleansed and scraped to a perfectly equal thickness—or thinness—in every part. Four sections are cut, each one shaped to form a quarter of a sphere. These fit neatly over the last layer of worsted, and inside the final covering of hard, strong leather, as a cushioning protection for the cork and worsted core. In the case of a match ball, every

[*Topical.*

Stitching together two quarters of the outer cover of a cricket ball.

By courtesy of]   [A. G. Spalding & Bros. Ltd.

(Left) Slugs placed in mould.   (Right) Slugs pressed into shape.

bit of material used has been weighed and tested time after time
during the process of building up the inner ball, to make certain
that the finished article shall conform to match requirements.

There remains the fitting of the strong outer cover of hide,
which, like the leather inner covering, is washed and scraped to
perfect uniformity of weight and thickness before being cut, mostly
into quarter spheres as in the case of the inner covering, and sometimes so as to form two halves, each of perfectly equal weight and
shaped to take the ball.   Then comes the final stitching.

When the ball covering is in quarter sections, each pair of
sections is stitched together on the inside, and examination of a
well-made ball will reveal the perfect join of these two, a line
running at right angles to the outer rows of stitching.   Now the
two halves are fitted over the ball with its soft leather covering, and
the final, outer stitching is done.

Examination of a match ball will show that there are no less
than six rows of this final stitching—that is, the stitcher goes round
the ball three times, each time making two rows, one on each side
of the joint.   Every stitch is perfect, taking an equal strain with
the rest and being of precisely similar size.   And there is the finished

ball, good for a few hundred "boundary" hits.

The making of tennis balls is a different business altogether, and is one in which machinery plays a very large part. For the main part of the ball, the very best of raw rubber is used, being either cut into "slugs" of which each is equal to half the rubber portion of the finished ball, or else cut into pieces after being rolled to the required thickness. Then each "slug" or piece of rubber goes to a mould which shapes it to its final form in

By courtesy of]   [A. G. Spalding & Bros. Ltd.

Trimmed shells being lined with flexible air retaining composition.

a temperature which vulcanises the rubber to its proper resiliency.

The edges of each half-ball are then shaped by machinery, and each pair is nearly—but not quite—ready to be cemented together.

To prevent the escape of air through the pores of the rubber, each half-ball is coated on its inner side with a special solution which closes all the pores and thus prevents escape of air from the interior of the ball after the final cementing. Again, the edges are levelled, and now the half-balls are ready to go to the moulds for the final process of cementing and inflating.

The fact that a tennis ball is inflated, or that the air inside it is retained at a higher pressure than that of the normal atmosphere, is one which even a good many players do not know. But it is so, for if the ball had only atmospheric pressure inside, it would be a lifeless thing compared with what it really is, and it is to maintain this pressure that the rubber is proofed against escape of air before the two halves of the ball are fitted together.

Now, with moulds containing the two halves of the ball exactly opposite each other, comes the cementing, which is neatly done by a machine through which the moulds are passed. Two small tablets inside the ball, which dissolve during the final cementing process, provide the gas which inflates the finished ball and gives it the necessary " life," or " bounce." With these tablets inside, each pair of halves is hydraulically pressed together, and the heat which vulcanises the rubber and cement into a perfect joint turns the two little tablets into the required quantity of gas.

These inflating tablets are prepared with the utmost accuracy, since the slightest variation in them would affect the internal pressure exerted and result in tennis balls of uneven "bounce." With the tablets dissolved after cementing, the balls go to " ageing " bins, in which they are left for a fortnight. At the end of that time a careful inspection is made of each ball to ensure that there is no leakage and that the correct internal pressure is maintained. Having passed this test (and any ball which does not pass it is rejected and scrapped), the outer surface is roughened with emery in readiness for the cloth covering,

By courtesy of]　　　　　[A. G. Spalding & Bros. Ltd.

Patent machine vulcanising cover to the core.

and now comes another series of tests to make certain that every ball is of a proper weight and size.

The final cloth covering is a specially-prepared fabric, which, like the rubber part of the ball, is tested in various ways to ensure its fitness. A rather intricate series of processes combines it with the ball, so that it will stand up to contact with the stringing of a

By courtesy of]   [A. G. Spalding & Bros. Ltd.

Finished half shells being placed in moulds and removed into vulcaniser for inflating and sealing.

tennis racket and still adhere perfectly to the rubber. The covers are cut from the prepared cloth by stamps, each ball requiring two pieces, and each ball with its two-piece covering is weighed to make certain that the whole, when fitted together, will be neither under nor over weight. After this the ball, covered with solution, has its cover fixed on lightly, and then the seams are machine-closed. After a final test, each ball is wrapped in a damp-proof cover and packed in its cardboard carton, or, if for export, in an air-tight metal container.

Photos by courtesy of]   [*A. G. Spalding & Bros. Ltd.*

Right hand side of picture shows cover being placed in position.   Those on tray show first operation.   Left hand side shows operation of closing the seam.

Finished balls being branded by means of a transfer before being packed.

HOW GOLF BALLS ARE MADE

THE centre of a golf ball consists of a small rubber bag filled with a weighted paste and tied with rubber thread. Around the centre or core is wound, by hand, a length of rubber tape. This process is called hand-binding. On to this hand-bound centre a further layer of rubber tape is wound by a machine. This is known as disc winding. Next the disc wound core has a length of rubber thread applied to it under tension, by machine. This is the process of thread winding.

The cover of the ball is made as a separate component and is stamped into discs from compounded gutta percha. These discs after stamping are in the form of half-spheres. The two spheres of the cover are placed on the core which is then put into a patterned mould. The resulting product at this stage is an unpainted golf ball bearing a pattern, name and markings, and having a saturn-like ring of excess gutta percha surrounding it. This excess is trimmed off by sharp knife blades and the ball is ready for painting.

Paint is next applied and the lettering and numerals on the ball are added by hand.

Filling bags with weighted paste and tying with rubber thread.

Winding rubber thread under tension on to the disc wound centre.

Photos by courtesy of]   *[Dunlop Rubber Co., Ltd.*

Trimming off the excess Gutta Percha cover.

Sir Adrian Boult conducting the B.B.C. Symphony Orchestra in the H.M.V. No. 1
Recording Studio.

MAKING A GRAMOPHONE RECORD

THE phonograph was the forerunner of the gramophone, and
the cylindrical phonograph records were first made by
people singing or playing directly into a horn, at the end of which
was a diaphragm carrying a needle, which indented the surface of
the cylinder. This meant that they had to speak very loudly, and
that only one record at a time could be made. Twenty years after
the invention of the phonograph, another inventor—Berliner—
realised that if he could record sound on a flat disc, it would be
easy for him to make a metal die from which he could press
innumerable other discs, in the same way in which a newspaper is
printed.

It is copies such as these and not, of course, the original record
which we buy in the shops to-day. Except for improvements in
detail of acoustic technique, no very revolutionary invention was
made in recording between 1877 and 1925. In this latter year
electrical recording and reproduction methods were introduced,
resulting in our being able to have far more lifelike reproduction.
Instead of singing or playing into a horn, the performer used a
microphone which converted the sound into small electrical impulses
which were led away to the recording room by cables.

MAKING A GRAMOPHONE RECORD

Let us go behind the scenes when a gramophone record is being manufactured and see exactly what happens. The recording studio is designed to afford the best possible acoustic conditions. Its acoustics have been carefully tested to ensure just the right amount of echo to make for naturalness. It is a very different room from the cramped little place where the first recording artistes had to sing into horns or instruments on shelves round the room. There is no necessity for a large orchestra to crowd round the recording instruments, for, if necessary, more than one microphone can be used. Indeed, when a singer is being accompanied by an orchestra, he has a separate microphone, while several other microphones can be used to pick up sound from the orchestra.

The orchestra is arranged to give a balanced sound in the microphone, and gramophone recorders no longer need to be afraid of a very large orchestra. The microphone can deal with the lowest notes of the drum as well as the highest notes on the piccolo. Before recording begins the piece has been carefully rehearsed and it has been ascertained that it fits nicely into the record, depending

Heat from the hot plate makes the " biscuit " plastic enough to roll it into a convenient shape, for insertion in the press.

MAKING A GRAMOPHONE RECORD

By courtesy of]   [E.M.I. Sales and Service Ltd.

The biscuit is placed in the centre of the press, which is then closed. The press first heats the material to make it mould perfectly, and then cools it. The disc is also cut to the correct size.

on the length and speed selected. Engineers in the recording room listen to the piece being played ; then, when they are satisfied that the arrangement of orchestra and singers is correct, the door is closed and a red light is shown just as in a broadcasting studio so that there shall be no unwitting interruption. The piece is played through and, if necessary, the recording engineers can exert a certain amount of control either on the volume or balance of the music.

The record blanks are made of specially prepared wax and it is essential that they shall be at exactly the right temperature while the record is made. For this reason the recording room is usually carefully heated and has a thermostat to ensure that the temperature does not fall below a certain point. In some instances the recording turntables are rotated by a system of pulleys and weights, this method ensuring a constant speed during recording. Today, normal turn-table speeds are 16, 33, 45 or 78 revolutions per minute, and this, of course, is the number of revolutions that the turn-table of your own gramophone at home should make. After the wax blank has been set on the turn-table, the recording head is lowered into the cutting position. A fine sapphire cutting stylus is used, as this is as hard as steel and less likely to become roughened. The cutting needle, or stylus as it is called, is made to vibrate from side to side by the magnified electrical impulses from the microphone(s) so that a wavy groove of constant depth results, the "waviness" of the groove depending on the nature of the sounds that are being recorded. As the recording turn-table revolves, so the cutting head is made to traverse the surface of the wax radially, to produce the long spiral groove.

When a record is being reproduced on your own gramophone, the needle follows the "waves" in the grooves and reproduces the original sound.

When a perfect record has been made, it is sent to the factory, where the wax is coated with metal and a negative made by electrolysis in a suitable bath. From this disc a few test records are made, and if these are found to be perfect, a positive is made from the "master." From this positive, again, a number of negatives are made and these become the dies or matrices from which the hundreds of records sold in the shops are produced.

These new records are made by placing plastic record material, together with the suitable labels, between two matrices or dies, which are mounted in a press. After the press has been closed, it is rapidly heated by steam, and then cooled by water. When the press is opened, the completed record is removed ready to play except for the fact that its edge has to be polished. Extraordinary precautions are taken in the factories to ensure that no dust or

By courtesy of]   *[The Gramophone Company Ltd.*
The completed record is removed from the press.

MAKING A GRAMOPHONE RECORD

By courtesy of]　　　　　　　　　　　　　　　[*E.M.I. Sales and Service Ltd.*

The wax is placed on the recording table and after adjustment of the recorder head the initial " run-in " groove is cut.

moisture settles on the metal dies before the records are pressed. If they did, imperfections would be present on the finished records.

Some of the great achievements of recording in recent years have been carried out on old records. In the early days of gramophones, many famous people including Florence Nightingale, Tennyson, and Mr. Gladstone made records. In most cases these records, where they could be found, were in a very bad state ; not that they had ever been very good by modern standards. By applying electrical re-recording, engineers reproduced the now long-dead voices from the old wax cylinders on to new discs, and these famous voices which were so nearly lost for ever, are now permanently recorded. In other cases early records made by such famous singers as Caruso have been re-recorded with a new accompaniment. Engineers ingeniously cut out the original accompaniment which, with the technical limitations of the time was necessarily very thin, and in its place inserted a new modern accompaniment with full orchestra.

While all these great improvements have been taking place in the recording studio, the reproducing apparatus has also been greatly improved. It is very little good, in fact, to have a record that is nearly perfect, unless the instrument of reproduction is also efficient. The latest methods of reproduction which have been incorporated into record players convert the vibrations picked up by the needle into small electric impulses. These impulses are similar to those which result from wireless waves being picked up and passed through a detector valve. They are taken to an amplifying valve and back into the loudspeaker. With medium- and long-playing records, sapphire and diamond needles, and high fidelity reproduction, the best records and record players really can bring perfect concert hall listening into our homes. Yet it was only fifty years ago when records were the shape of jam jars! Gramophone records form a large part and a very popular part of broadcast programmes. In the special studios used for gramophone broadcasts, the records are not playing aloud, the electric sounds being carried direct from the pick-up to the amplifying and broadcasting apparatus.

A final check and polish and the records are packed for despatch to the shops.

An airport control tower.

HOW AN AIR LINER IS NAVIGATED

IMAGINE that you are about to set off on your first flight. You have already been seen by officials of the Customs, Health, and Immigration Departments. You are at the airport, walking over the concrete " apron " towards the air liner. Now you have boarded the aeroplane. Now the engines are droning away, the throttles are pushed wide open, and you are racing down the runway, rapidly gaining speed. Then, almost without noticing it, you are airborne.

As this is an imaginary flight, you can now leave your comfortable seat and come into the cockpit at the front of the aeroplane, which is, of course, " out of bounds " to passengers. Here you will meet the aircrew—the men who fly the aeroplane. There will probably be five of them : the Captain, First Officer, Navigator, Radio Officer, and Engineer Officer.

Let us meet the Captain first, as he is the most important person on the aeroplane. He is as much in command as a sea Captain on a ship—and he is just as much responsible for the safety of his passengers and crew.

The Captain's duties began before you reached the airport. His first job was the vital one of deciding whether this flight was to take place at all. An hour or more ago he went with his crew to the Meteorological Office to study the weather charts and hear what the experts had to tell him about the probable weather conditions along his route. You can imagine from this that the Captain must know a lot about meteorology himself. When he had been informed of all the facts and forecasts, he had to make his decision whether to fly. It was up to him alone. If he said the weather was not good enough, no one could order him to make the flight.

However, modern navigation is so scientific that the weather has to be very bad indeed for the Captain to make an adverse decision. To-day, as you know, he decided to make the flight, and the aeroplane was prepared.

Of course, the routine maintenance work had already been

[B.O.A.C.

Passengers in an air liner.

The air crew on the flight deck.   [B.O.A.C.

carried out. The aeroplane is inspected by engineers every twenty-four hours, and special checks are made also after every landing and before every take-off. All these checks are most thorough, and are made in a definite order. A separate test was made to ensure that the system used for cooling each engine was working properly; another test was made on the hydraulic system which raises and lowers the flaps and undercarriage; each engine was thoroughly tested to ensure that the running was " sweet "; fuel and oil leads and the many electrical connections were all examined separately. Nothing was left to chance.

Now the Captain, after giving his decision on the flight, checked the documents showing the load that the aeroplane would carry, and made sure that the loading was correctly carried out. Your weight was included in the figures for the load.

When you boarded the aeroplane the Captain and his crew were already preparing for the take-off. There are two seats in the front of the cockpit, and the Captain sits on the left-hand one. The reason for this is that when landing by a single flare-path at night, the aeroplane touches down on the right of the flares, which the Captain can thus see through the port window.

Just before the take-off the Captain is in his seat, in radio communication with the Control Tower of the airport. He is wearing headphones and speaks into a hand microphone. The apparatus is arranged so that he need merely press a button when he wants to speak, and release the button for the set to go on to "receive." The Captain cannot taxi or take off before he receives permission from the Control Tower.

[B.O.A.C.

The captain in his seat at the controls.

Now let us look round the cockpit. Our first impression is of a bewildering array of dials, gauges, buttons, etc. Leaving these for the moment, you will see that in front of the Captain is the control column. It is a bit like the steering wheel of a car in appearance. The control column moves backwards and forwards, while the wheel or half-wheel on it can be rotated to left or right. The Captain's feet are resting on two pedals. The control column and the pedals are the main controls of the direction of flight of the aeroplane.

One of the dials tells the Captain the speed of the aircraft. When this reaches a certain figure, the Captain pulls the control column gently towards him. This raises the elevators, which are hinged horizontal flaps attached to the tail-plane ; the action of the elevators depresses the tail of the aircraft, and so the nose comes up. When it is off the ground the Captain holds it steady for a few minutes, to gain airspeed ; then he pulls the control column again, and the aircraft starts to climb. Meanwhile he has already touched a switch which brings up the undercarriage, the wheels folding up behind the engine nacelles.

Up the aircraft flies, until sufficient height has been gained. Then the throttles are eased back, and the aeroplane cruises smoothly on an even keel.

Before we go any farther, let us consider how an aeroplane, which is so much heavier than air, is kept in the air. The explanation is that the air flowing past its wings and body surfaces exerts a lifting force. The aircraft is designed so that the air passing underneath exerts more pressure than the air over the top, and this causes an upward lift. It follows that when the aeroplane increases its speed, it tends to rise higher, and the pilot has to apply his controls to keep it on a level keel. This he does by pushing the control

[B.O.A.C.

Flight deck of a Stratocruiser.

column forward, thus lowering the elevators and making the nose point downward. The same procedure is necessary for losing height in preparation for landing.

We have said that the wheel or half-wheel on the control column can be rotated to the left or to the right, and the control here is on the ailerons, which are hinged flaps set in the back edge of the wings. With the movement of the control column one aileron turns upward and the other downward, and this movement tilts the wings to the left or right. The ailerons, then, are needed for turning to the left or right, and the pilot moves the control column according to the direction in which he wants to turn.

An aircraft makes a turn at an inclined angle, like a bicycle going round a corner, and this tilting of the wings is called banking. In certain turning movements banking alone may suffice, but in general turning also calls for the use of the rudder.

We mentioned earlier that the pilot's feet rest on two pedals, and these control the rudder, which is placed at the tail of the aeroplane and moves to the left or right on vertical hinges.

It must not be imagined that the pilot uses these controls only when he wants to change the direction or height of the aircraft. All the time the aeroplane is in the air it has to be controlled. You cannot just set it on a course and let it fly by itself. However slight the wind, it would soon dip down on the wing, or fly nose-heavy ; and it keeps on an even keel only because the pilot is correcting these tendencies all the time.

To save him from heavy manual work, the pilot has a metal box on his right hand, and by adjusting certain knobs and wheels—called " trimmers "—he can have the work of control carried out for him mechanically. An even more wonderful piece of mechanism is the automatic pilot, known as " George." This instrument operates by means of gyroscopes, which remain rigid in space while spinning, and it can carry out the work of the pilot while he has a rest. " George " has to be watched, however.

So far we have talked of the Captain and the pilot as though they were the same person, and in fact the Captain is the senior pilot ; but he is very much more besides. His authority is not just nominal, and he has to know the jobs of all the rest of the aircrew. As may be imagined, the training for this job is long and thorough, and the tests are stiff.

HOW AN AIR LINER IS NAVIGATED

Seated on the right of the Captain is the First Officer, or co-pilot. He takes over the controls when the Captain needs a rest, or wants to leave the cockpit to stretch his legs and, probably, go into the passenger cabins to chat with you and me.

Now let us meet the other members of the aircrew. First of all, here is the Navigator, who keeps the aircraft on its proper course.

[B.O.A.C.

Control officials giving instructions to the incoming plane.

This is no easy matter, because it does not depend only on the direction in which the aeroplane moves. There is almost always some wind, and this affects both the speed and the direction of the aircraft. If it is blowing directly from behind at, say, forty m.p.h., then it will increase the aeroplane's speed over the ground by the same amount ; if it is a head wind, on the other hand, it will reduce the ground speed, as it is called, correspondingly. If it is blowing from either side—and it nearly always is, to some extent—then it will blow the machine off its course. The Navigator has to make allowance for this from the start, and check the correctness of his allowance all through the flight.

HOW AN AIR LINER IS NAVIGATED

The Navigator, like the Captain, started his job before the flight began. He too studies weather reports, and was supplied with special forecasts of the winds along his route at certain heights. From these he worked out his flight plan, giving the compass course to be followed and the air speed required to achieve a certain ground speed.

This flight plan was based on forecasts, and throughout the flight the Navigator has to check that the course is correct. The compass tells him the direction in which the aircraft is headed, and another instrument tells him the speed through the air. From his knowledge of the speed and direction of the wind he can calculate the ground speed and track—that is, the path over the ground which the aircraft is following. If he is out of his course he must work out a new one.

Before he can do this, the Navigator must find the position of the aircraft over the ground. This is called getting a " fix," and can be done in a variety of ways. One method is by map-reading. The Navigator studies the ground below, picks out objects like bridges and churches, and identifies them on his special map. But this alone would be insufficient for navigation, as the aircraft may be flying over the sea or a desert, or it may be night-time, or clouds may make it impossible to see the ground. So the Navigator has to know other ways of getting a fix.

There are several of these. One method is the sailor's way of " shooting " the stars with a sextant. Radio and radar provide other aids, which can be used at daytime or at night. The Navigator uses every means to get as many fixes as he can—and once he has got a fix he has to calculate quickly what alteration in course should be made. Unless he is quick the aircraft will have travelled so far past the point of the fix that the new course is no longer of any use.

Now let us meet the Radio Officer, who is also busy throughout the flight. His equipment includes radio telephony and wireless telegraphy. The former is used mainly by the Captain and for inter-crew communication. It is used when near an aerodrome— as when the Captain speaks to the Control Tower at the time of take-off and landing. Wireless telegraphy is used during the rest of the flight, communication being by the Morse Code. The Radio Officer has to listen to weather reports, and transmit the position of the aircraft. He also calls up ground stations to get a bearing, and uses his own " Radio Direction Finding " equipment for the same purpose. Towards the end of the flight he will get into contact with the aerodrome and receive signals telling the Captain the final course to be followed.

Finally, there is the radar equipment, which is used in conjunction with radar beacons on the ground. With the aid of this the pilot can " home " on a beacon. When landing in bad

[B.O.A.C.

A ground station giving a bearing.

visibility the Captain may need his radar set to find out for him when he is in line with the end of the runway. The radar navigation equipment is usually operated by the navigator, and the radar blind landing aids by the pilot.

The last member of the aircrew whom we must meet is the Engineer, or Flight Engineer. He is responsible for the operation of the engines, in the same way as an engineer on board a ship. He has to keep a constant watch on the fuel consumption.

The other members of the staff on our air liner are the stewards and stewardesses, who make the flight comfortable and enjoyable. They give a standard of service unequalled in any other form of transport. Their main job is supplying food and refreshments, and catering on an air liner is an art in itself.

Time, like our aircraft, flies, and already we are nearing our destination. The Radio Officer has made contact with the aerodrome, and we have been given permission to enter the circuit at a certain height. To explain this we must leave the aeroplane for a moment, and take a peep inside the control tower.

When several aeroplanes are approaching one aerodrome, and visibility is bad, so that aircraft must be brought into the landing circuit one at a time, then the control officials adopt a system known as " stacking." Each of the incoming aircraft is told to circle the aerodrome at a fixed height, and there is usually 1,000 feet between these heights. As one machine lands, each of the others is directed down to the next height ; and so our aircraft goes down in steps of 1,000 feet, until it reaches the lowest safety height of 2,000 feet, which is the last before landing. Then comes the message that it is all clear to land.

Visibility is good to-day, and landing is quite easy. (Visibility was one of the things that Flying Control told us about when we first got into radio communication with them). But we should know that our aircraft is fitted with a " blind landing aid," operated by radar in conjunction with marker beacons ; and, also, that by watching us on a radar screen the ground staff could, if necessary, " talk " the Captain right down on to the runway.

Just before landing our Captain touched a switch, and the under-carriage went down, a green light telling him that it was securely locked. Then out went the air-brakes—long strips of metal to lessen our angle of descent. Then, with scarcely a bump, we were down on the tarmac.

Our flight is over. The Captain makes his report and hands over the " Technical Log," which is nothing less than a complete record of the behaviour of the machine throughout the flight. From this, the engineers will attend to any tiny fault that developed while we were in the air. The Technical Log is of vital importance to the men whose responsibility for our safety in the air is no less than that of the aircrew themselves, although we never see them at work : the ground engineers of the maintenance staff.

[L.N.A.

Loading up vegetables and fruit in Covent Garden.

HOW A GREAT CITY IS FED

SUCH a simple matter to get a meal in a big city ! There are dozens of hotels and restaurants and cafes all waiting to serve you, or you can buy your food at any one of hundreds of shops, which all have new supplies arriving at regular intervals. Modern organization of trade and transport makes it possible for city-dwellers to eat as conveniently and cheaply as the people who produce the food.

Take your milk, for instance. It was obtained many miles away in the country, but it reaches your table in town as fresh as if the farmer had just brought it in from the dairy. Large city companies buy the milk under contract from thousands of farms, collecting it several times every day by motor lorry. It is taken to the local centre, where it is chilled ready for its journey to the city.

Sometimes the churns travel in ordinary goods vans on the railway or the milk may be piped into special glass-lined tanks so

41

carefully insulated that the temperature does not change during transit either by road or attached to an express train. Soon the milk arrives at the distributing dairies, which are situated at various points on the outskirts of the city in a " ring " arrangement. Pipes suck it out of the churns or the tank, and you do not see it any more until it reaches the bottle, for, to ensure the utmost purity, all the processes are carried out in completely-enclosed vessels or pipes.

Samples of the milk are taken on its arrival, expert chemists examining it in a great laboratory and submitting it to microscopic, chemical and bacteriological tests. As soon as the samples are pronounced standard, the milk is frozen to an icy temperature and then mixed in huge glass-lined containers to give uniform quality in every bottle. Then it is pasteurised, a safeguard which makes it absolutely impossible for any germs to exist, by first being heated to 145 degrees Fahrenheit and kept at that temperature for half an

By courtesy of]   *[Sunbeam Photo Ltd. & Weston Bros. Dairies Ltd.*

An automatic bottle filling machine in operation.

Conveyor system for unloading bananas.

[*Fox Photos.*

hour. Finally it is swiftly chilled again and is then passed along to the bottle-filling machines.

The bottles reach the filling platform on an automatic conveyor, which brings them from the washing-machine where they have just spent forty-five minutes in a series of sterilising fluids. They pass under the fillers, are swiftly capped and emerge to be packed into crates and taken off by fleets of motor vans to local dairies all over the city. From these the milkmen deliver the bottles to the consumer's doorstep. Large consumers such as hotels will have their milk delivered in special churns, and these, too, are sterilised and filled by machinery in the same way.

Then there is the fruit—you can obtain any variety you fancy from the city shops all the year round. For the rapid distribution of quickly-perishable things like fruit and vegetables, every city has its great central market, which opens for reception business at midnight, when convoys of motor lorries arrive bringing the produce gathered in the country gardens and orchards earlier in the day. Some lorries come from the docks, since nowadays much greengrocery is imported—apples from Canada, oranges from South Africa, cabbages and lettuces from Spain, tomatoes from the Canary

[L.N.A.

Unloading sides of meat from a refrigerator hold.

Isles and so on. It travels in special refrigerated compartments built low down in the ship's hold for the minimum of movement, and as soon as the ship berths, the cases are shot down a chute directly on to the vehicle waiting to take them to market.

Expert porters quickly unload all the lorries and stack up the contents in the open stalls of the various wholesale agents to whom the growers have consigned them for sale on commission. When there are numerous boxes in a single consignment, of pears maybe, one box will be opened and a few pears taken out and placed on a plate alongside so that the buyers can judge their condition without any trouble.

At five o'clock in the morning the market opens to its customers, who include the retail greengrocers, the catering buyers from clubs and hotels, etc., and the humble street-hawkers. They all have vehicles waiting near at hand and as soon as they have made their purchases in the sales, which are conducted on the auction principle, the market porters carry off the goods and load them on to the vans to be driven away to the shops and kitchens.

HOW A GREAT CITY IS FED

Much the same procedure takes place at another huge market in the centre of the city, where meat and poultry are sold. Soon after midnight the supplies start pouring in from the country by rail and road, travelling in hygienic zinc-lined containers with plenty of ice to keep the meat cold and fresh. Quantities of frozen meat brought from the Dominions and the Argentine also arrive from the docks.

Smocked and hooded porters work swiftly, getting out all the carcases, some of which are slung across from lorry to stall on small but powerful cranes. Then the white-coated butchers cut up the meat into halves and quarters, often using electrical hand-saws on a conveniently long flex that is plugged into the nearest power-point. There are mechanical choppers, too, and low wooden trolleys on which the meat can be wheeled about the spacious stalls with the minimum of effort.

Sea food also figures prominently in the diet of a big city, but

Huge supplies of fish laid out for sale at Aberdeen fish market.

45

the central market where fish is distributed does the whole of its daily business in a few short hours. Supply loads do not begin to arrive until half-past four in the morning, but these boxes and crates are all ready for sale. They bear tickets which give full particulars of their contents, so that the buyers can make their purchases without examining the fish inside.

As the fishing boats come back to port with their catch, representatives of the sales agents in the city market are waiting on the quay and as each skipper lands his baskets of fish, these men judge the qualities with expert eyes and buy on the spot for their employers. The fish is then cleaned and prepared in buildings adjoining the harbour and packed with ice and salt ready for its journey to town by rail or road. If the city to which it is going possesses docks, then the fish may be loaded again into a special carrier motor-vessel which takes it round the coast with speed.

At the city fish market, the buyers arrive on the heels of the supplies. Their vans and carts wait in the vicinity and as they make their purchases, the fish is carried out by the market-porters, who wear peculiar leather hats, rather like an outsize in sou'westers but with a gigantic peak back and front. This affords them very necessary protection, for they carry the fish on their heads and the boxes are naturally oozing melted ice—as well as being saturated with the water that was hosed over them at regular intervals to keep the contents fresh while they were standing.

Then, of course, there is the bread which is eaten in such gigantic quantities in the city. Scores of big bakeries work day and night all the year round providing the thousands of loaves required every day. They obtain their flour from large milling companies, who, in turn, purchase the grain direct from the farmers.

Some wheat is grown in Britain and as soon as it is harvested, the farmers take samples to the local Corn Exchange where the milling company's agents examine it and make their offers according to the quality. Most of the grain comes from overseas.

All the big docks are now equipped with special apparatus which sucks the grain direct from the hold of the ship by pneumatic elevators. It is carried along and sent down a chute into immense iron "boxes," in which it is automatically weighed and is then passed on to be fed into sacks, which also find their way to the granary store.

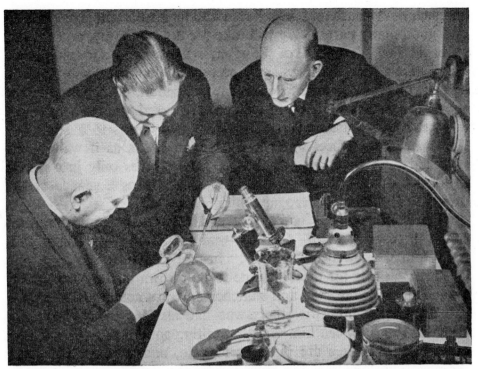

Finger-print experts at work at the Yard.

THE MACHINE OF A THOUSAND USES

THE power station of the machine is situated almost under the shadow of the Houses of Parliament, and its name, Scotland Yard, is world famous. The machine itself is known as the Metropolitan Police Force, and it has, literally, a thousand uses, all designed to make life and property safe, to prevent crime, and to protect the ordinary law-abiding citizen.

All these activities interlock with one another: for instance, a " smash and grab " raid by criminals, in nine cases out of ten, means that a car has been stolen somewhere for use by the thieves, and left abandoned somewhere else. Thus the police engaged in traffic control, in tracing this car, are also engaged in the detection of crime. The whole Police Force is one great machine, and your safety on the road or in your home is the proof of its efficiency in working.

There are so many parts to this wonderful machine that it is impossible to mention them all, but description of a typical—though imaginary—" smash and grab " raid and its results will give glimpses of a good many parts. We will take for the scene, say, an ordinary street in the West End of London, with women shopping, men going about their business, and everything looking quite peaceful and normal in the middle of a fine afternoon. A powerful grey sports car, with four alert-looking, well-dressed young men, draws in to the kerb outside a jeweller's shop, and comes to a standstill. The man at the wheel lights a cigarette, and sits as if waiting for somebody. A uniformed constable, passing, sees only just such a high-class car as often stops in this street, takes a glance at the driver and, failing to recognise him, passes on.

The policeman has got to the end of the street and vanished round the corner, when—Crash !—and splintered glass tinkles as it falls from the jeweller's window. Instantly, one of the men who had been waiting for the big stone to be thrown at the glass thrusts a hand through the hole and snatches up trays containing the most valuable rings, while two others, who had also leapt out of the car, clear the way between him and the waiting sports car. In a matter of seconds, all three are in the car again, and it is on the move, the people in the street too stupefied by the suddenness of it to do anything. But a plain-clothes detective belonging to the police division in which this street is situated—not a " Scotland Yard " man—has seen from a distance what was happening, and he hares off to the nearest telephone box and dials " 999." The operator gives him " Police " and he is soon speaking to the Information Room at Scotland Yard, the nerve centre of the Metropolitan Police communications system.

Now hear his report, which tells the value of police training.

" Detective Smith speaking from call box in Blank Street. Smash-and-grab raid occurred one minute ago at Jones and Robinson's jewellery shop here in Blank Street. Car used, sports Lagonda, grey tourer. Registry XPA 632. Driver, young man in blue serge jacket and soft grey hat—I didn't see his trousers or face. Three other men concerned. One middle aged in dark grey suit, soft black felt hat, medium height and rather stout. One tall young man, in light grey flannel suit and grey cap—quite six feet tall. One slender young man, blue serge suit, brown soft felt hat, brown shoes. All four quite well dressed. The car disregarded traffic lights and is headed westward up to moment of telephoning. Oh, the middle-

NEWSPAPERS POURING THROUGH THE PRESS

TILTING A BUS

In accordance with police regulations, the chassis must reach an angle of 28 degrees without the bus overturning.

aged one is dark and foreign-looking with a hooked nose—his was the only face I could see across the street before they went away."

In an incredibly short time, even before the detective has finished reporting all the facts, all police cars fitted with wireless sets and cruising in that section of the Metropolitan area—which stretches for miles in all directions beyond London limits—are getting a wireless call, about the crime, and all police stations, too, are warned

The Map Room at Scotland Yard.

by teleprinter. But, even so, the grey car is a fast mover, and by this time is probably well away from the scene of the raid.

Now comes in a report from one police station to say that the owner of XPA632 has just reported his car as missing from outside a house at Dalston, where he parked it two hours before. He does not know how long it has been missing, but left it with the ignition locked and took the key away with him. And that, as headquarters knows, gives the habitual criminal very little trouble : a practised car thief usually carries a full set of ignition keys.

Information Room now know for certain that the car used is

stolen. The progress of the chase is plotted on large maps and additional cars are called and directed to strategic points as reports come in from the pursuing vehicles.

Ignoring all traffic signals and taking incredible risks, the grey car had got out on the bye-pass, only to be sighted by a police car, which gave chase at once. And, though the grey car was fast, police cars of the type that chased it are faster. Four determined officers waited for their car to draw alongside the grey fugitive, the one at the wheel edging in toward its running board—and then a pistol shot rang out and one of the officers lay back with a bullet through his shoulder. But another police car ahead, drawn across the road, put an end to the chase. With locked wheels sliding, the grey car came to a stop, the four criminals leaped out and took to their heels, only to be captured and taken in, identified and charged with the crime.

Their finger-prints told the names which they themselves refused to give, for all four had served sentences and were in the records of finger-prints, of which Scotland Yard possesses 10 million—a figure which is added to at the rate of 40,000 a year. Since all four carried pistols, and all denied shooting the wounded constable, the bullet which had wounded him was microscopically proved to have come out of the barrel of one particular crook's pistol, and a second charge of attempted murder was put against him. The owner of the grey car was told where to find it, and the stolen jewellery held as an " exhibit " until after the trial of the four, when it was handed back to its owners.

Now this hypothetical case shows not only police in action, but the working of their wireless system, which enables the mobile squads to " get on " to a crime of the kind in such an amazingly short time. Then there is the perfect co-operation, shown in the speed with which the theft of the grey car was reported and the watch kept by all patrolling cars. Had the crooks got away, their descriptions would have been circulated. The Yard keeps not only a name index but also a method index—recording characteristic ways in which crimes are committed by certain crooks as well as their names.

Detectives would investigate the haunts and whereabouts, in this case, of known smash and grab thieves who usually carried guns, for example. Detailing men to go and investigate the haunt of criminals likely to have been concerned is a commonplace with

THE MACHINE OF A THOUSAND USES

The Information Room—nerve centre of the Metropolitan Police communications system.

the detective section of the police force: so much so, in fact, that a detective looks in at some of these haunts every evening to see if any known character is missing, and, in the event of one being missing while a burglary or other crime is committed, that one is marked down for investigation. Among other qualities, the police have long memories and a good eye for faces, and a man who has once served a sentence ranks as "known to the police," in more ways than one.

Crime detection and prevention, however, is only one branch of police activity. You may see a uniformed constable on duty shepherding school children across a road and holding up the traffic for them: a little later, he may be taking particulars of a car smash, for which he must know all the Highway Code for drivers, and he may be giving first aid to some injured man or woman while waiting for the ambulance which he has summoned to appear. Next, you may see him controlling traffic at a road junction where traffic lights have not been installed, or he may be taking a lost dog to the police station, where it will be well cared for until its owner, traced by the name and address on the collar, appears to take it away. A royal procession passes through the streets, and the broad back of the policeman keeps back the crowd within limits, and next day, if an old lady tells a policeman that she wants the Bank of England, he politely directs her to it, instead of telling her to take it away.

In uniform, always courteous and obliging : promoted to " plain clothes " work, just as courteous, but concerned more with criminals, the enemies of society, than with ordinary people, and keen at his work, patient enough to " keep his nose down " on a case till he has tracked down and arrested his man : either way, one of the guardians of some eight million people, and part of the great machine acknowledged to be one of the best police forces in the world.

By courtesy of]   [J. Arthur Rank Orgn. Ltd.

A film " criminal " escapes.

Director instructs actor how to write with a quill pen.

HOW A FILM IS MADE

IN these days we all take the sound picture or "talkie" for granted but not everyone fully understands how it is that the shadows of the actors and actresses on the screen are made to speak.

Of course, it is not the actual voice of the actor we hear but only its mechanical reproduction. It is, in fact, a photograph of the voice we hear, just as it is a photograph of the person that we see. The sound of a film is generally recorded quite separately from the pictures. A microphone, or more often microphones, are hung in suitable positions in the studios and pick up the sounds—whatever they may be—the voice of a singer, the sound of a river running over stones, or of horses galloping towards the winning post. Reflectors are often used to catch the noises from moving objects.

In these days the sound record is usually made on a film, although at one time the sounds for many films were recorded on records, like those we play on a gramophone. The sound is converted by the microphone into variations of an electric current and these variations of current are made to open and shut small " valves " through which a light of constant intensity is focused on to a sensitive negative that is being run through the apparatus at a constant speed. The markings on the negative when it is developed, therefore, represent variations in the electric currents, which in themselves correspond to variations of sound. In some cases the current changes are made to light a lamp with varying degrees of brilliancy, but the main principle of changing sound to light markings on a film is always the same.

Afterwards, the sound-track, as this film is called, is printed on to the edge of the picture film which has been taken, a portion having been masked in readiness.

In general practice the sound-track is not placed exactly opposite the picture which was being taken while the sound was recorded. This is because in the reproducing machine, or projector, the films have to pass first in front of a light which deals with the part we

By courtesy of]   *[J. Arthur Rank Orgn. Ltd.*
Taking a close-up of the science master conducting an experiment.

A technician recording the sound.

see on the screen and then later through a " gate " in which the sound is reproduced. Very careful adjustment is necessary to ensure that the picture and its correct sound appear exactly together and, of course, the reproducing machine has to be synchronised with the recording machine. The reproduction of the sound is the exact opposite of the recording. A light is projected through the sound-track and focused on to a photo-electric cell, which has the property of recording variations in light in terms of an electric current.

This electric current is amplified very greatly, taken by wires to the back of the stage, where it enters loud-speakers at exactly the moment when the right picture is appearing on the screen.

Since the introduction of " talkies " in 1928, the principles have remained the same. The great improvement in the accuracy of the sound is due to improved technical methods. In the early " talkies " the range of sound which could be recorded was very limited, but improvements in microphones and in loud-speakers, as well as in the acoustics of the cinemas themselves, have brought the sound nearer to perfection. The problems of the " talkie " engineers have been great. At one time it would have been useless to record either the lowest or the highest notes, because no loud-speakers could have reproduced these frequencies. Quite a good balance has now been struck and it is doubtful if any improvements designed

By courtesy of]   [M.-G.-M.
A film editor checking a scene on his " movieola," a miniature motion picture theatre.

to bring an even wider range into use would be well worth while, for the human ear has definite limitations in its range.

An even later innovation than the " talkies " was the modern colour film, and nowadays nearly all our first-feature films—and many others—are photographed in colour. Colour films had been known for many years but these were usually rather crude, and a further objection was their increased expense. Now there is more than one process for making films in natural colours which give realistic results and cost little more to make than the ordinary

(*Above*) Photographing a bullfight.

[*Columbia Pictures.*]

(*Below*) Shooting a film from a sandstone cliff.

[*M.-G.-M.*]

black and white type.   Lighting still presents some difficulty.

The troubles of coloured film making are very much those of coloured photographs, except that the cinema demands only a standard form of white light to give colours through a colour film. But there are the further difficulties that in any colour film, more light is needed in the studio and very much greater light from the projector.

Another complication is that of copying a film.   The reel which is used in the projector at a local cinema is not that taken in the studios at Elstree or Hollywood.   It is usually a print from this film and anything from fifty to two hundred copies may be made of a popular film.   This is simple while it is in black and white but much more costly when colours have to be introduced.

In principle a coloured film is generally made by separating each of the primary colours with screens.   In the case of still photography it is not very difficult to take the same picture over again using a different screen, but with a moving picture the screen has to be incorporated in the film itself.   In the Kodachrome process

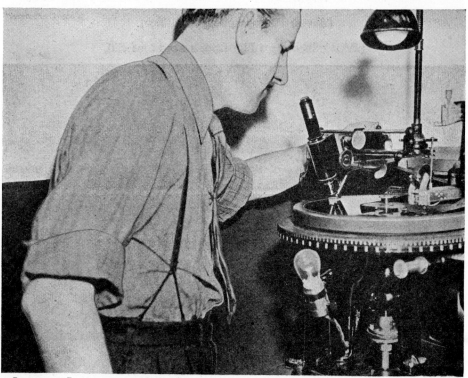

By courtesy of]   *[M.-G.-M.*

Recording sound on a wax record.

By courtesy of] [*M.-G.-M.*

Photographing a scene from a " Western."

there are three layers of emulsion, one of which is sensitive to red, another to green and another to blue, layers of gelatine absorbing the colours that are not wanted in each case. In development, this composite film has to pass through three separate processes, one for each colour.

There are other systems, in one of which the colour is obtained on ordinary black-and-white films by the use of filters. In most cases the problems involved are very technical and difficult for those who are not experts in optics and dyeing to appreciate. One method, used in films which are not subject to a high degree of magnification, is to incorporate numerous prisms in the film. These are of almost microscopic dimensions and are used to break up white light into colours in conjunction with a special attachment to the lens.

In the 3-D cinema, two views are thrown on to the same screen, one almost exactly over the other, and arrangements are made

The actor discusses the next scene with his director.

so that only one of them will be visible to each eye.   This is achieved
by showing one picture in green and the other in red, and issuing the
audience with spectacles containing one red glass and one green glass.
The eye with the red glass over it is able to see only the green picture,
and the eye with the green glass only the red picture.   The audience
then sees a picture with a convincing three-dimensional appearance.

But the use of these strong, contrasting colours is both wasteful of
light and tiring to the eyes, and in one of the best modern systems
polarized instead of coloured light is used.   Polarized light is light
in which all the vibrations are taking place in the same plane, and it
will pass through certain crystals only when the crystals are held in
the right position.   The two pictures are thrown on to the same
screen as before, but each is shown in light polarized in a different
direction.   Spectacles are worn as before, but their special lenses are
not coloured; they contain polarizing crystals arranged so that the
light from only one picture can pass through each lens.

HOW A FILM IS MADE

Another system of 3-D employs a screen consisting of thousands of narrow glass rods, which direct the two pictures one to each eye without the use of spectacles at all, but this is not very satisfactory except for people sitting in or near the centre of the cinema. "Wide-screen", in which the suggestion of space is created by having the audience partly surrounded by an enormous picture, with the sound coming from different directions, is not genuine " 3-D " projection, but a substitute for it.

The system that provides the greatest impression of realism at the present time is known as Cinerama. With Cinerama, three synchro-nised projectors throw images on a huge curved screen and the sound comes from seven loud-speakers. The cost of installing Cinerama is generally prohibitive—about £20,000 per cinema—and very few cinemas are suitable for conversion. Wide-screen systems like Cinemascope and VistaVision are far less costly and without doubt the most practical and popular.

By courtesy of]   [M.-G.-M.
Assembling lens mounts for use in motion picture cameras.

CATCHING WILD BEASTS ALIVE

IN the depths of the Malayan jungle a black leopard prowled suspiciously around a tempting bait of fresh meat. For five nights in succession the leopard had circled restlessly in range of the bait, but something seemed to warn the animal that if he touched it he would be sorry. But on this night hunger was stronger than caution. The black leopard made a dive for the meat.

In doing so the huge beast touched a trip-wire with its foot. The movement of the wire released a wooden peg. A bamboo grating dropped with a crash. With a snarl of rage the black leopard whirled round, only to find that it was trapped.

"We've got him, boys !" shouted an excited voice.

A white man, who had been patiently watching the leopard from a hiding place in the jungle now hurried forward, followed by a gang of native hunters, who dragged a wheeled cage stoutly built of logs. The white man was a collector of animals. He had been commissioned by a zoo to obtain a black leopard, "fully grown and in perfect condition, with flawless teeth and no blemishes of any kind." After five days of waiting he had made his capture. But his work was by no means ended yet. The trapped leopard was hurling itself about in mad savagery. Somehow it had got to be transferred from the trap to the cage.

The cage was drawn up close to the trap, and a door was slid open. But the leopard refused to enter. It crouched back, tail lashing, eyes sparking. The hunters brought long poles with which to prod the black leopard into the cage. The great beast went into a rage, biting at the poles, and snapping them off.

But at last it was driven into the cage. It threw itself against the bars, spitting and screeching, lashing out with its sharp claws. The bars of the cage shivered at every onslaught, for the leopard weighed as much as a full-grown man. The cage was hung on long poles, and coolies carried it to the nearest village, where it was put on a motor lorry, which carried it to the nearest dock.

When the animal collector arrived at the dock, he was faced with fresh trouble. The native dock labourers were terrified of the snarling leopard, and refused to take any part in loading it on board the boat.

Undaunted, the collector called upon his own native hunters to

help him.   After a great deal of struggling, the captive was hoist
on board.   Its cage was lashed on deck, not far from the cook's
galley.   This proved to be a disastrous mistake.

The voyage began.   The ship was only a short distance from the
shore.   The leopard, maddened by the smell of fresh meat which
was coming from the cook's galley, crashed all its weight against
the bars of its cage.   The collector ran to the spot, to see what could

[Fox Photos.

A wild elephant trapped in a pit.

be done to calm the angry beast.   But he arrived too late.   There was
a smashing sound.   The cage collapsed.   Spitting with fury the leopard
dragged itself out of the cage backwards and stood on deck, free !

The members of the crew stood in a semi-circle, not daring to
move, waiting to see what the leopard would do.   It seemed to
hesitate, then with a wild screech it took a mighty leap over the side,
and dived into the water.

It began to swim strongly towards land, but suddenly one of the
native boys cried out :

" Look, tuan, sharks ! "

CATCHING WILD BEASTS ALIVE

It was true. Sharks were swarming to the kill. The leopard, though so terrible on land, stood no chance in the water. Nothing could be done to save it, and the collector could only watch in horror and dismay when the sharks attacked and killed the animal he had gone through so much to capture.

The work of collecting wild creatures for zoos and circuses, and the arduous business of bringing them home after they have been caught, forms one of the most dangerous professions in the world.

Big game hunters are fond of boasting of their prowess, but the man who collects animals alive shows much more pluck and daring, since he uses firearms only as a last resource, and must employ every means possible to avoid harming his quarry. He does a useful work, too. He helps to preserve rare specimens of wild creatures, while the big game hunter is ruthlessly wiping them out.

Each kind of animal must be caught in its own special way. Polar bears, for example, are lassoed by hunters in canoes. Usually three or four canoes are tied together. As soon as the bear is roped, it swims away for all it is worth, dragging the canoes in its wake until it is tired. Then the men in the canoes get out their paddles, and tow their captive back to shore, where he is put into a cage.

Giraffes are usually hunted on horseback. Fully-grown giraffes are as a rule left alone, because, being anything up to eighteen feet high, they are almost impossible to transport for long distances. They are too tall to go under railway bridges. Generally, young ones, up to ten feet tall, are caught.

Boa-constrictors, and other big snakes, are taken captive after they have had a good meal. The boa has the power to unhinge its jaws so that it can enlarge its mouth to three times its normal size. In this way it can swallow an antelope in a single mouthful, but it takes about ten days to digest its meal, and during that time it is so sleepy and sluggish that it can be handled without danger.

Poisonous snakes are caught with a lasso, or with a forked stick which is used to pin them to the ground by the neck so that the hunter can pick them up by the tail.

The chamois, a kind of mountain goat, is very difficult to deal with because it is so nervous. When caught it is liable to hurt itself in its struggles to escape, so the hunter prepares a kind of stretcher, well padded with a bed of moss and ferns. The chamois is tied down on this stretcher, and carried down the mountain side.

Big birds, like ostriches, are chased on horseback, and lassoed. The ostrich is such a foolish creature that, once caught, it is only necessary to pull a sock over its head and it can be led anywhere by two men, each holding one of its wings.

A Tiger caught in a special net.

Every animal provides the collector with special problems. Many of the creatures become sulky in captivity, and go off their feed if they cannot get their natural foods. Condensed milk has been found to be the best thing to restore their appetites.

An anoa, a rare kind of water buffalo, proved a big problem to one collector. When turned loose in the compound, it fought any other animal within sight. It tackled antelopes twice its own size, and beat them. It seemed to be absolutely fearless. But one day the collector heard the anoa crying out with fear. He went to investigate, and found the animal shivering with fright, terrified by the presence of a harmless little porcupine !

One of the great diamond mines in Pretoria, South Africa.

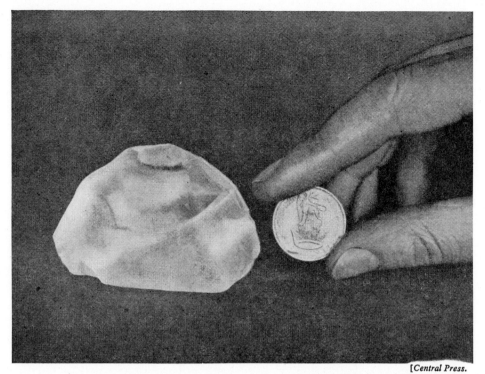

The Junker Diamond, found by a poor farmer in South Africa, compared with a shilling. It is worth more than £100,000.

WHAT ARE JEWELS?

JEWELS are merely stones which are highly prized for their beauty and rarity, and they come from many different parts of the world. All jewels but one are minerals, like any other rock ; but the one exception, the pearl, is the most valuable of them all. Because of that, and the fact that it is in almost every way different from the others, the pearl must come first. Men have travelled far, and undergone great hardships in the search for other jewels. They have to risk their lives diving, often in shark-infested waters, for pearls.

Pearls, it is often said, are the tears of oysters, the deposit of lime with which the oyster slowly surrounds and covers an annoying particle which has got inside its shell. Sometimes, man takes a hand in pearl production by supplying the oyster with a suitable piece of grit on which to work. Such pearls are known as " cultured pearls " ; but although it takes an expert or X-ray to distinguish them from the real thing, they are not so valuable as those which the oyster makes on his own. Most of the finest natural pearls come, nowadays, from the Persian Gulf, although rare and valuable black pearls come from Venezuela, and there are important pearl fisheries in many other parts of the world, including Ceylon and some of the Pacific Islands.

All other jewels, as has already been said, are really pieces of rock, most of them being unusually hard, and either shining brilliantly or being beautifully coloured. Even the emerald, ruby, sapphire and precious opal are only exceptionally beautiful varieties of quite common minerals. The emerald, for example, at present the second most valuable gem, is believed to owe its beautiful green colour to the fact that it contains a minute amount of the metal, chromium. And the deep royal blue of a fine sapphire is probably due to a rather more rare metal, titanium.

What we call brilliance in a gemstone is caused by its unusually great power of bending light. The practical result of this power is that once any light has got inside such a gemstone, it is difficult for it to escape again into the outer world. It may, therefore, be reflected several times inside the stone before reaching the surface at an angle at which it can make its escape. This means that from whatever direction a diamond is illuminated, it will throw out light in many directions. So, from whatever angle one looks at it, a diamond will always appear to sparkle.

Fire means the flashing from the stone of light of different colours, as the head is slightly moved. This also has to do with the capacity of the stone for bending light, but in rather a different way. Ordinary sunlight, or white light, consists of a mixture of lights of all the colours of the rainbow, and when these enter a gemstone, they are split up into their different colours. A gemstone therefore possesses fire according to the extent to which it bends light of various colours differently. A diamond, for example, is not only more brilliant than any other gemstone, but shows all the colours of the rainbow when viewed from slightly different angles.

Because gemstones are both hard and heavy, they are often found in river gravels. Being hard they can stand being knocked about, and being heavy they are more likely to collect on the bottom of the stream than are any of the lighter fragments of stone. Most sapphires, rubies and topaz are found in gravel, as well as an appreciable proportion of diamonds, beryls and a number of other stones.

This native mine in Burma is one of the richest producers of rubies in the world and has been worked for centuries.

69

WHAT ARE JEWELS?

In the great South African workings, diamonds are sought, like emeralds and opals, by regular mining operations. They are found in a soft blue rock, which powders and turns yellow when it is exposed to the air. Workings are at first open—that is to say, they take the form of great pits, in one case as much as six hundred and sixty feet deep. Usually, as in any other mine, underground workings have to be begun at much lesser depths, when shafts are sunk and galleries run out to tap the diamond-bearing layers in the normal way. Formerly, and this was a peculiarity of diamond-mining, the soft blue rock used to be left to crumble, when it had been got to the surface, so that the diamonds could be extracted from it without crushing. Nowadays, however, corrugated rollers are used, and the rocks are crushed without risk of damage to the diamonds.

Yet the mining of diamonds, and indeed of other precious stones, by no means completes their story. It has already been mentioned that diamonds owe their brilliance to the reflection of light round and round within the stone. Because of this fact, the cutting and polishing of diamonds, so that they can be shown off to the best advantage, is a highly-skilled occupation.

The " brilliant " cut of a diamond produces a stone with as many as fifty-eight different faces, and there is another " cut " with as many as eighty-eight. Nor are all these faces visible. In the " brilliant " cut twenty-five of the fifty-eight faces are on the under-side of the stone. Yet the angles and sizes of all of them must be perfectly cut if all the light entering is to be ideally directed.

The first operation is the removal of any flaws in the stone. It is split in pieces to get rid of these, a notch being first cut with another diamond and the job completed with knife and hammer. Further cutting is carried out with metal discs, covered with diamond dust to give them hardness and oil to hold enough of the diamond dust in position. A similar mixture is used in polishing the cut stones on each of their many faces, machinery being employed to provide the power in both cases. Yet the work is no less skilled ; for, although a machine may supply the power, the necessary judgment is supplied by the man who works it. And if no other stone presents quite as much difficulty as the diamond, the cutting of none of them is a job which an amateur could hope to undertake.

A microphotograph of crystals in the grain of an aspirin tablet. They resemble delicate seaweed.

WHAT PHOTOGRAPHY CAN DO

EVER since Niepce, Daguerre and Fox Talbot invented photography more than a hundred years ago, many new tasks for the camera have been discovered. It is doubtful whether the men and women who posed so stiffly before the early cameras could have dreamt that one day photography would be possible in the dark.

Photography in the dark is one of the most interesting of comparatively recent advances, although it was used scientifically in 1917. Ordinary photographs depend upon the action of the light rays of the "visible spectrum" upon chemicals contained in a gelatine coated over a plate or film. But in addition to this "visible spectrum," the æther waves by which we see things in colour, there are other waves to which our eyes are not sensitive. A little shorter than the shortest visible light waves are ultra-violet rays, the rays which tan us at the seaside, and rather longer than the longest visible light waves are infra-red rays. There are also the very short X-rays, which have properties all their own, and the wireless waves which vary in length from a few centimetres to twenty miles.

These light waves are all very much of the same kind ; that is to say, they are of the nature of electromagnetic waves and differ only in wavelength, somewhat in the same way as the lowest note produced on a piano varies from the highest.   Now, although we cannot see X-rays, infra-red, or ultra-violet light, the camera is more accommodating than the eye.   The invisible waves affect chemicals in much the same way as the visible waves, and by development we can make the images clear to our eyes.

Very spectacular results have been gained by using infra-red rays. These light waves are less than one seven-thousandth of a millimetre in length, and it is only within the last 20 years that a simple dye has been discovered which will make a photographic plate sensitive to them.   By cutting off all the white light from a lamp by means of a filter, it is possible to take a photograph in the dark.   The sitter can see nothing, but the special plate in the camera is sensitive to the invisible infra-red light and records a picture.

A very dramatic demonstration of taking photographs in the dark was made some short time ago when a cinema-camera was focussed on a stage which was apparently in total darkness.   I say apparently, for although the audience could see nothing, the players were bathed in infra-red light.   Someone was murdered in the play, and the audience heard a scream, but it was only when the film in the cinema camera had been developed that the audience was able to see the " murderer."

Infra-red rays are emitted by hot objects and therefore it is possible to take a picture of, for example, a hot iron, entirely by the light of its own " heat."   To the eye it seems that the iron is perfectly invisible, but the eye of the camera, with its wider range, takes in the infra-red rays.

Infra-red photography is not primarily concerned in taking pictures, except for special purposes, although it has made it possible to take pictures of photographs being developed in a photographic dark-room, a feat which would have been impossible twenty years ago.   In this case the photographs being developed were not, of course, infra-red.

The great value of infra-red photography lies in the fact that infra-red waves are very much less absorbed by dust, smoke and fog than are the other parts of the spectrum.   As is well known, the redness of the setting or rising sun is due to absorption of the other

WHAT PHOTOGRAPHY CAN DO

This special finger-print camera is used in the detection of crime.

With a spectroscopic plate, a nebula 7,100 light years away can be photographed.

Photos by courtesy of]

Thousands of documents can be recorded on a reel of film.

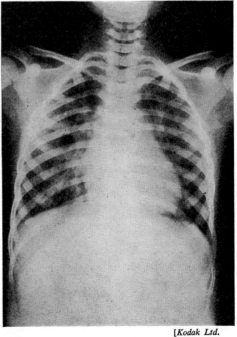

[*Kodak Ltd.*

Every hospital has an X-ray department, where photographs such as this are taken.

colours of the spectrum by the dust and moisture in the air ; but the fog-penetrating power of infra-red waves is even greater than that of visible red waves.

In the majority of instances, disappointing results are obtained when taking a photograph of some beautiful view from a mountain top. Generally, the foreground is clear, but mountains in the background are blurred and indistinct. This is not a fault of the camera, but merely that the light reflected from the distant objects is mostly absorbed before it reaches the lens. Take the same scene using a plate or film sensitive to infra-red rays, and there is an enormous difference. The mountains six or eight miles away which appeared so misty will stand out boldly. Again, it is difficult to obtain clear landscape pictures during a slight drizzle, but with the help of infra-red plates the results almost compare with those given in bright sunlight.

Using plates sensitive to infra-red rays and very fine apparatus, a photograph has been taken from a balloon showing the horizon 330 miles away. Indeed, it seems that the only limit to the distance at which photographs can be taken is the natural curvature of the earth. Infra-red photographs have shown us big cities as we have never seen them before. The infra-red rays penetrating the fog and dirt which hang like a pall over every town, even on the finest days, have proved that we might have glorious views of buildings from distant hills, if only smoke could be abolished.

In aerial photography, infra-red rays are invaluable, for they enable clear photographs to be taken from great heights, whereas with ordinary plates a great deal of detail is lost owing to light being absorbed and scattered by dust and moisture in the air.

When infra-red photographs are examined, it is found that they appear rather different from ordinary pictures. The object of the maker of a photographic negative has generally been to render the colour " values " in the negative as near those of the eye as possible. We say that red is a " bright " colour, but in an ordinary photograph it comes out rather dark. By using a panchromatic film, that is a film in which correction is made for colours, red objects appear much brighter in relation to, say, yellow. In infra-red photographs trees appear almost white, because the green leaves reflect infra-red rays very well.

Photography by X-rays is not now a novelty, and every hospital

A view of the Thames at Henley taken with infra-red plates.   The trees appear to be covered in snow.

Photos]

The same scene photographed on an ordinary plate.

has an X-ray department. But many people do not know that there are very many applications of X-rays in industry, apart from medicine. X-ray photographs are now taken of pieces of steel which are to be used for important parts of machinery and the radiographs show immediately the smallest flaw which may be hidden deeply in the metal. Through one of these photographs it may be, for example, that an axle intended for a railway coach or aeroplane is rejected, a flaw having been seen. If that flaw, quite invisible to the naked eye, had not been found, an accident might have resulted. Golf balls are photographed under X-rays to see if they are perfect, while another application of X-ray photography is to examine the genuineness of pictures.

The use of X-ray photography for this latter purpose is best explained by describing what happened when a certain old master was photographed. The picture showed a man holding up a wine glass. But an X-ray photograph showed what was underneath the surface paint and that the wine glass had originally been a bone which the person had, apparently, been gnawing. Someone had painted over the bone, but this might never have been known but for X-ray photographs. In the same way, hundreds of other pictures have been found to have been altered, and the use of X-ray photography in the examination of old masters is now general. These photographs have proved to be of first importance in establishing the genuine nature, or otherwise, of many famous pictures.

Ultra-violet and infra-red rays have been used in a similar way for examining documents. Old manuscripts of which the ink was so black and smudged that they were barely legible have been made clear. In one interesting case, whole lines of an old book had been blocked out in black by some censor who evidently did not approve of their contents. By infra-red photography it was possible to show what was written underneath the blacking out and readers knew for the first time for three hundred years what the author had really written. Forgeries on cheques, or alterations of documents, have been detected in exactly the same way, and to-day the camera is a very valuable ally to the detective. It shows him stains which are not apparent to the naked eye and more than one difficult case has been solved by photography.

The eye of the camera can be very quick, and this fact has also recently been turned to use. In many sporting events there have

A MICROFILM READER.

Documents recorded on microfilm are viewed on this instrument, which projects an image of the document the size of the original or larger. The Reader can also be used to produce copies of the original forms, without a dark room.

been disputes, such as whether a goal was fairly scored or a boxer really fouled. Photographs have in some instances settled these arguments, although generally too late to affect the result. Now has been developed a special camera which will photograph the end of a sprint race and give a picture in two or three minutes. With this camera acting as judge there can be no question whether the race is a dead heat or whether one contestant won by two inches.

For high speed record breaking by aeroplanes the use of a camera in connection with a clock

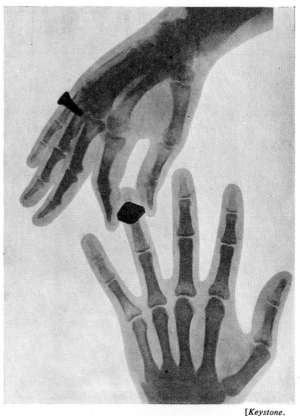

[*Keystone.*

An X-ray of hands, with rings on the fingers.

is now made compulsory by the international rules. The apparatus used is intricate, but in principle the camera photographs the aeroplane as it crosses the mark, and a picture of a chronometer also appears. A number of photographs are taken at each end of the course, but only the picture in which the aeroplane is actually starting or finishing counts, and the exact time is shown on the negative. The two cameras may be electrically connected so that they are perfectly synchronised. In this way a degree of timing accuracy that would be absolutely impossible by hand is achieved; this is very important in cases where an error of one-fifth of a second, almost negligible at speeds about 60 m.p.h., makes a great difference when speeds are in the neighbourhood of 1,100 m.p.h.

High speed photography has also been used to study lightning. Lightning travels much too quickly for the eye to receive a real picture of it, and specially constructed cameras have recently shown that a lightning flash is very different from what was supposed. Instead of coming down in a single spark as it appears to the eye, lightning may travel backwards and forwards several times. The camera also showed that after a flash the air remained illuminated for 1-2,000th of a second, and it was possible to measure a speed which varied between 14 and 180 feet in a millionth of a second. The cameras used for this kind of photograph are quite different from those we use for snapshots. They have many rapidly revolving lenses.

Similarly elaborate cameras have been used for photographing explosions. When a spark occurs inside the cylinder of a motor engine, there is an explosion, but this explosion is not instantaneous. It travels like a wave down the cylinder. Photographs taken in thousandths of a second have shown us this effect, and made it possible to see exactly how the combustion wave travels. It is not, of course, possible to photograph the invisible gases, but their shadows are recorded with ease.

Although photographic negatives are now vastly better than was the case twenty years ago and tones of all the different colours can now be reproduced quite well, colour photography is still difficult and seems likely to remain, for the moment, outside the range of the amateur who does not want to trouble with elaborate developing or printing processes. There are now available,

[*Keystone.*

Recording the fall of a drop of milk and the splash it makes, which at the height of its rebound looks like a crown.

however, colour films which can be sent back to the manufacturers for developing. To make a print, it is necessary to use three negatives, each of which deals with one of the colours, red, green or blue. Three negatives are made, and three prints are taken on carbon tissues, each of which is impregnated with a colour complementary to the primary. These have to be transferred to a support, the process is not only laborious, but calls for a high degree of skill.

Of other uses to which photographs can be put, only a few need be mentioned. Photography can reveal distant stars which are quite invisible to the eye, even with the telescope. It can also tell us something of the conditions on other planets. It can give us microscope enlargements up to 80,000 diameters. By aerial photographs we can produce in a few days maps which formerly took years to make. With all these wonderful advantages there is little doubt that the science and art of photography have still to see many improvements within the relatively near future.

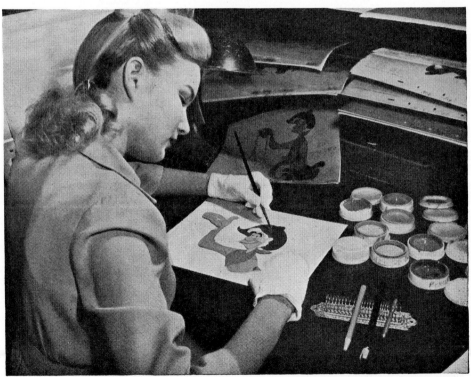

An artist putting the final touches to a drawing of Walt Disney's " Pecos Bill."
But for the development of film photography, it would be impossible to make a cartoon film.

A back somersault recorded by means of high speed photography.

By courtesy of] [A. V. Roe & Co. Ltd.

A GIANT WIND TUNNEL.

It is now possible to reproduce flying conditions at very high altitudes and at speeds faster than the speed of sound for test purposes.

Buses parked in the garage after the day's work.

A NIGHT IN THE LIFE OF A BUS

IF you were to stand outside one of the great garages of a road transport undertaking one evening between 10 o'clock and midnight you would see a steady procession of empty motor buses returning after their long day out at work.

Travel stained and dirty, they go inside and are handed over by their service drivers to the maintenance staff who will prepare them for the morrow's operation. Let us see what happens to a bus after its busy day in the streets.

The driver's work is soon finished. All he has to do is to go to the office and enter on a sheet which will show the number of the bus he has been driving, his remarks on how it has been running and any mechanical adjustments he thinks are needed. The conductor also has this to do in regard to the body, for bells, lighting bulbs, windows, seats and other body fittings can become defective or require adjustment just in the same way as the engine or mechanical parts of the bus, which are regarded as the driver's concern. The conductor has more to do however. He has to pay in the money he has taken and account for tickets he has sold. His waybill shows this both in total value of tickets and the quantities of each kind sold.

The waybill is a most important document, for it gives the fullest details of everything the bus has done. The conductor enters on it his own and driver's names, the service number and particulars of the bus, the number of his ticket punch and the letters and number of the various classes of tickets in his ticket-box when he set out. At each terminus he also enters the numbers of the top tickets in his ticket-rack. Each ticket is issued by a ticket-punch which records and should agree with the tickets accounted for as having been sold.

The punch is much more than a means of cancelling the tickets. It contains a miniature "cash-register", which is set at zero when the conductor goes on duty, so that when he finishes, it gives the number of the tickets he has sold. All the little round pieces clipped from the tickets fall into a special chamber inside the punch so that they may be counted and reckoned up according to their different colours for different fares if any difficulty should arise in balancing the conductor's money.

After the driver and conductor have left the bus the garage staff take it in hand. First it is driven on to the fuel pump and its fuel tank refilled and its engine oil replenished for the next

By courtesy of]   [London Transport Executive.

Disinfecting the interior of the bus.

By courtesy of]   [London Transport Executive.

The garage day staff giving buses a complete overhaul.

day's running. Whilst this is proceeding, the used tickets, rubbish and dirt that is on the floors is removed by enormously powerful vacuum cleaners. This is done by passing large flexible long rubber pipes, which are connected to the garage main suction plant, through the windows and entrances or up the staircase and moving them over the floors, sucking up the dirt, tickets and rubbish in the process. They work very similarly and are in fact very large versions of the vacuum cleaner that you have in your homes. The bus is then moved along to be washed and disinfected and to have its radiator refilled. It is washed in a special area of the garage which has high pressure flexible hoses connected to piping in the roof. These hoses are used in conjunction with long handled soft brushes to clean down the sides, the front and back and the windows. The men are clothed to protect them against wet and the area of the garage is suitably drained to prevent water running everywhere.

When the bus has had its high pressure bath, it is shunted away into a position which will enable it to be moved out in the morning, at the time and for the route for which it will be wanted, with the least possible disturbance to other buses. To take care of this a garage parking plan is used.

The windows are polished and the metal work such as the radiator and handrails cleaned and the interior disinfected. The mechanics will attend to whatever reports the driver has made and although he may have reported everything in good running order, the bus is still closely inspected in case any defects not easily seen may be likely to develop. If a defect is found which requires still further investigation, the bus is put over a pit before it is due to go out and the item rectified or alternatively it is withdrawn from the day's service for the day staff to repair.

As its time to go on service approaches, its route, faretable and destination equipment is checked for the service or services which it is to run. Its tyres are examined and pressures checked and if these require inflating, a portable compressed air cylinder which is carried on a trolley is wheeled up and connected to the tyres. The cylinder has been previously charged from a main air compressor plant in the garage and the task of blowing up a tyre amounts to a few seconds only. The bus must be ready to leave punctually so the engine is started and warmed up for a few minutes previously. Bus engines are heavy and a little reluctant to start in cold weather, particularly Diesel engines and to assist them to start and to relieve the strain on the bus batteries an auxiliary or booster starting set, as it is called, is used. This consists of a pair of batteries mounted in a portable trolley which is wheeled alongside. A socket connection is provided which enables the power of these batteries to be used in addition to the bus batteries and when the self starter is pressed, the engine is revolved much more briskly and consequently starts more easily.

The bus is now ready for its driver again but apart from its nightly routine it is withdrawn from daily service periodically so that it can undergo complete lubrication, tests and renewals of various parts.

On these occasions the day staff at the garage deal very systematically with the bus. The chassis parts will be lubricated under high pressure and the oil drained and renewed in the engine, gear box and rear axle. The brakes, steering gear, springs and wheels very closely examined. The fuel system must be cleaned, the electrical system examined for short circuits or potential defects and batteries recharged, the hydraulic or air pressure and vacuum

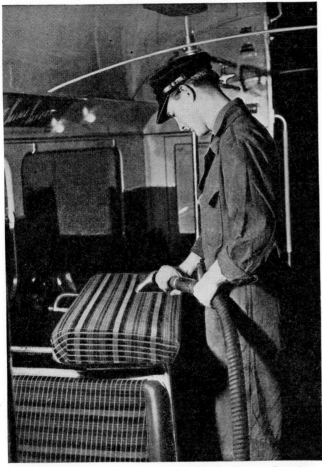

Removing dirt from the cushions with a powerful vacuum cleaner.

systems examined for leaks as they all play an important part in the vehicle in starting it, controlling it and stopping it. It also gets a more detailed cleaning on these occasions, the interior roofs and paintwork is washed with soap and water, and the exterior roof washed also. The cushions are vacuum cleaned. The wooden floors and staircase treads are treaten with a preservative and quick - drying stain and the exterior paintwork touched up to present a nice fresh appearance.

But the bus has a very heavy daily task to perform and it must be completely overhauled occasionally apart from the attention it gets at its garage. This is also periodically done and it is sent to a works for this purpose where the body is removed and the chassis stripped entirely.

The chassis frame is first steam cleaned and subjected to a close examination for cracks or distortions and then is gradually re-assembled with new or reconditioned assemblies and parts. The works are equipped with many varieties of machines that will weld, turn, drill or bore metals in the many forms and shapes that are required. Electrical crack detecting apparatus is used to test the front axle beam and steering parts. Electrical machines test the wiring circuits of self starter and dynamo. The wear in engine cylinder bores and on crankshaft journals is measured accurately by special gauges. Machines to test fuel and petrol consumption, machines to test road spring deflection, the amount of wear in ball bearings, the wear or deformity in the teeth of geared mechanisms ; all these and many more are used at the main works in overhauling the chassis.

The body is renovated at the same time. The main structural parts being renewed if necessary, the floors relaid and the staircase rebuilt. The outside panels and the mudguards will be replaced, the windows reglazed and the operating mechanisms overhauled and then with newly upholstered cushions and a complete repaint and retrim inside and out, the body is remounted to the chassis and with new wheels and tyres and a thorough test the bus is once more fit to resume its daily activity.

But this is a little apart from its nightly routine and we left the bus at the garage at the stage where its nightly toilet and preparation for daily service has been completed and it is now ready for its crew again.

The driver and conductor report for duty and " sign on " on a sheet provided in the garage offices. The driver obtains the number of the bus he is to drive and proceeds to examine it, satisfying himself that such things as the brakes, steering gear, windscreen wiper, hooter and controls generally are in satisfactory condition. The conductor meanwhile obtains from the office his equipment including that tin box which you often see and which is so important to him. This contains enough tickets and a log-card for the day's operations. Whilst on weekdays each ticketbox is used for two days, on special occasions and on Sundays a one-day box only is required. These tickets come from the printers in parcels of a thousand, and each, as you will often have noticed for yourself, has the number preceded by two letters.

Clean and fresh, the bus presently leaves for its long hours of duty on the roads. The conductor enters the time of leaving the garage on the new log-card he has just been given for that day and then puts down the time again whenever he arrives at a stage-point and ends or begins a journey. The bus is expected to arrive and leave at set times which have been calculated by the officials of the transport undertaking so that the buses are consistently timed and run at definite intervals all day long. Obviously, it is best for

passengers and everybody else concerned when one bus comes to
the stopping-place at ten minutes past, another at twenty past and
a third at half-past the hour rather than one should arrive at five
minutes past with the other two appearing on each other's heels at
twenty-five past.

When there is anything such as a big traffic " jam " which holds
up the bus on the road and causes it to reach the terminus late,
then the conductor must also make a note of all the details on his
log-card and get the driver to add his signature in confirmation.
In fact, when you come to think what a lot of clerking the conductor
has to do, not to mention always giving the right change, ringing
the bell and telling people how they can get to their destination,
and seeing that nobody tries to travel farther than the stage to which
he has paid his fare, you will probably decide he is undoubtedly a
man of character still to be able to come along and say, " Fares,
please," with such a cheery smile.

By courtesy of]   [London Transport Executive.

A bus washing team at work.

HOW TO DRIVE A CAR THROUGH A TREE !

This is a simple trick if you happen to be in Underwood State Park in California, where many of the giant redwood trees have been cut in this manner at the base.

HOW YOUR HOUSE IS BUILT

WHEN you have chosen the plot of land on which to have your new house built, the architect comes along to inspect it and to make what is known as a survey. He needs to learn many things before he can begin drawing his plans. For instance, he considers the slope of the land and the nature of the soil—perhaps it is inclined to be damp and so will need to be drained by means of deep trenches running into the cinder-filled pits before the foundations can be laid. He notes which side of the house will be most exposed to the weather and arranges for protecting eaves or some protection to break the wind's force that way. He also decides what kinds of building materials are best suited to the local climate and the neighbourhood.

When the architect has drawn his plans and the local Council have approved them and you have agreed the estimate, then the builder and his men get to work. First they clear and flatten down the ground on which your house will actually stand and carefully measure out the size of the foundations. This space is excavated and filled with a substantial layer of concrete, which is stone, sand, water and a cementing or binding ingredient mixed into a soft mass and then allowed to dry, when it becomes strong enough to support tremendous weights.

[*Mirrorpic.*
Labourers carrying up bricks on their " hods."

91

The first few layers of the bricks that will make the walls are fitted into the cement all the way round so that the weight of the finished structure will be evenly distributed. Extra piers are put at the corners and under the places from which the chimney stacks will presently rise.

The bricklayer fastens his bricks together with wet mortar, which may be made from either lime or cement. Each row of bricks that he lays he refers to as a " course." First he builds up the quoins, or angles, of the house six or eight courses high and after he has got these absolutely straight and true, he proceeds to lay the same number of courses for the lengths of the wall between. For the quoins he uses his square and spirit-level and other tools to ensure perfect accuracy, and then between the quoins he stretches a line, perhaps of string, the exact height of the next course he is going to lay.

[Mirrorpic.

Bricklayers laying a " course."

Laying drainage pipes.

Brickwork must not be carried up too rapidly lest the mortar " gives " under the weight before it is properly hardened and throws all the courses out of accuracy. So the bricklayer only carries up three or four feet of the wall at a time and works evenly all round the house instead of building it up one complete wall after another. He follows the outline of the rooms as indicated by wooden strips laid by the builder who, in turn, gets all his instructions from the blueprint of the architect's plan, which sets them out in full detail.

The chimney-stacks are built inside the walls of the house so that none of the heat will be wasted outside. Most of the better-built houses have two separate outside walls, with an air space between them, to give greater protection from the weather. One wall is built immediately inside the other, joined by iron struts or bars cemented between the bricks at intervals for better reinforcement.

As soon as the walls are up, the joiners arrive. They provide the framework for the roof, rows of wooden rafters fastened across each other and over which the slates or tiles are placed in rows and secured with mortar. Under the roof the joiners lay a level floor of thin planks, and this becomes the ceiling for the top rooms of the house.

They make the ground-floor over the foundations, putting stout planks all round the brick supports already there and then laying the floor-boards over these. Thus an empty space is left between the floor and the actual foundations, which makes the rooms warmer and drier than if the floors rested directly on to the concrete and also provides accommodation for the water, electric light, gas and other domestic pipes to pass through from the house to their respective mains outside.

Carpenters at work on the floorboards.

For while the joiners are working, the plumbers and electricians and other specialists are also busy. The service pipes and wires that must travel upstairs are carried up the wall, of the kitchen maybe, and then taken along underneath the boards that will provide the bedroom floors, to emerge, perhaps, in the bathroom. When the kitchen ceiling is put up, laths are placed across under all these pipes, etc., so that they are completely hidden from view and the laths are then neatly covered with thick layers of wet plaster, or plaster board, which is white-washed when dry to make the plain flat ceiling we know.

The inner walls of the house are covered with heavy cement plaster, which securely embeds all the pipes. Meantime the joiners are putting up the wooden staircase frame and fastening the tread-boards on it and placing the door-frames into the spaces that have been duly left in the brickwork, to which the frames are joined with special putty. Fireplaces are installed, generally arriving direct from the manufacturers ready in one piece and only requiring to be cemented on to the chimney stack. Window-frames are fitted into their " gaps " too. Nowadays they are often made of metal treated so that it does not corrode, or shrink in extremes of weather and loosen the panes of glass, which are affixed with putty. There is generally some protection so that the glass is not directly exposed to wind and rain. Perhaps there will be an eave or a little " rim " just above or a draining sill running beneath, or the window may even be fitted back into the brickwork instead of being flush with the wall of the house.

You can have the outside walls adorned in various different ways. Parts of them may be covered with cement and then painted, or they may be studded with ornamental tiles or squares of fancy stone. Soon the decorators are at work, inside and out, adding the final touches to your new house.

Fixing the metal piping encasing the wires of the electric installation.

Photos by courtesy of]   [*The Postmaster General.*

(*Above*) A postman clearing a pillar box.
(*Below*) Postmen sorting correspondence in a " travelling post office."

Passing letters through a stamp cancelling machine.

HOW A LETTER REACHES YOU

WHEN you affix the stamp to your letter and drop it into the pillar-box across the road, you are commanding the services of the largest department of Her Majesty's Government. Well over a quarter of a million people are employed every day all over the British Isles in running the gigantic organization which, with the least possible delay, will deliver your letter at the place to which you have addressed it. To avoid delay, however, it is important that your letter should be clearly and correctly addressed.

Very soon the postman will unlock the pillar-box with its individual key from his big bunch, and slide the letter into his bag. When he has emptied all the pillar-boxes along his particular route, he takes the letters in his bag to the local Sorting Office, and tips them out on to a long table, called a " facing table."

The first operation is to separate the correspondence into three classes : letters of ordinary size, which are called short letters ; large letters, known as long letters ; and packets such as newspapers and bulky documents. The letters are arranged by the postman with the addresses all facing the same way. One day an inventor may succeed in making a machine to place letters with their addresses all facing the same way, but for the present this is an operation which has still to be done by hand in every Post Office in the world.

From the facing table the letters pass to the stamp-cancelling machines, some of which work at the rate of seven hundred a minute. The letters pass upside down into the machine, and the postage stamp in the corner is cancelled by a die, which impresses the place of posting, the date and the time. This machine has a clever recording device to show how many letters pass through it.

Now that the postage stamp has been cancelled, the letter is ready for its journey in the post. It goes to a primary sorting table where there is a framework usually consisting of forty-eight boxes or compartments, each labelled with the name of a large town or a county, or a group of counties. For instance, if your letter is going to a city such as Birmingham or Manchester, the sorter puts it into a box bearing a corresponding label. Letters in these boxes travel direct to the office of destination, along with the thousands of other letters which a large town like Manchester or Birmingham receives several times a day from Sorting Offices all over the country.

Air services are used to carry bags of mail quickly between some large towns in the British Isles, but the Post Office sends most of its correspondence by ordinary passenger train. It maintains a number of special trains called " Travelling Post Offices," which carry only mails, and on which the correspondence is sorted when the train is travelling at speed. There are, of course, many points along the route of the train at which mails must be delivered and others taken on board.

It would not be very quick if the train were to stop at every point, so to save valuable time bags are exchanged at specified places along the line by means of a clever mechanical apparatus. The apparatus consists of iron arms attached to the carriage, one on each side of the doorway ; the mail bags, enclosed for protection in a leather pouch, are suspended on a stout strap. A large strong net at the side of the railway track receives the pouches from the train, and the train collects pouches by means of a similar net attached to the carriage.

At every stopping place along the route, mail vans await the

By courtesy of]   [The Postmaster General.

The clever device by which mail bags are collected and delivered.

arrival of the Travelling Post Office and take the bags of letters to the Sorting Office of the town. The largest Sorting Office in this country is at Mount Pleasant in London, and it is also one of the largest Sorting Offices in the world. It deals with some three million letters every week-day. As the despatch of this immense amount of mail matter through the streets of London would cause great traffic congestion, much of it is sent by the Post Office Underground Railway, which connects a number of large Post Offices in London with several of the railway termini. These Post Office trains have neither drivers nor guards, being electrically controlled by a single operator from a cabin.

When the letters arrive at the Delivery Office, they are sorted yet again. This time the bundles are taken out of the mail bag, unfastened and sorted into another of the forty-eight box frames, but now each box is labelled with the name of a postman's " walk," as his delivery route is called.

When the final bundle has been thus sorted, the contents of each box are taken out and passed to the preparation tables, where the postmen prepare the letters for actual delivery. This stage consists in sorting the correspondence into boxes bearing the names of the roads and streets in which a postman delivers, and arranging the letters in order of delivery. That order may be according to the numbering of the houses at which he will call, and in any case he will deliver so that he need make as few crossings as possible. If he is serving a large block of flats, he puts the letters for the highest floors on the top of his pile, so that he can ride straight up in the lift and then deliver the letters to the floors below as he walks down.

The postman puts the newspapers and bulky packets loose in his pouch and then ties all the letters into bundles of convenient size. If you examined these bundles, you would notice that a letter was sticking out here and there. This is to indicate when the postman has a newspaper or other bulky packet to deliver.

And now there remains only the actual delivery. If you were at one of the large postmen's offices when a delivery was about to begin, you would see a stream of postmen setting out, each with his load of letters, post-cards, circulars, and packets. Soon all this correspondence will have reached its destination, heralded by the postmen's well-known " rat-a-tat."

By courtesy of [[*The Postmaster General.*

Loading mail bags into the port hold of an aircraft.

By courtesy of]

[The Postmaster General.

A tray conveyor at Mount Pleasant sorting office in London.

(*Above*) Photo writing (retouching) on the gloss negative of a map.

(*Below*) The monotype process camera used in map making.

By permission of]　　　　　　　　　　　　　[The Director-General, Ordnance Survey.

Map-makers taking levelling observations.

HOW MAPS ARE MADE

IF you are keen on maps, but not so deeply in love with Euclid, it may help you to remember that his arguments about triangles are very useful indeed to map-makers. If the earth's surface were all perfectly flat, dry ground, other methods might have been adopted, but in view of the frequency with which accurate measurements have to be taken over hilly or mountainous country, or even over the sea, it is extremely useful to know that by measuring the base of a triangle and the angles at each end of it, one can determine the exact position of the apex.

In setting out to make a map of a strange country, therefore, the first step is usually the preparation and measurement of a convenient base. The base may be several miles long, but the most extraordinary pains are taken to measure it with the greatest degree of accuracy. A special tape is used, made of a metal called " Invar," which has the property of expanding or contracting only very slightly with changes of temperature. From this base observations are taken towards different points, which become the apex points of triangles. By joining these apex points a longer base is established ; and further observations are taken, so that a whole system of triangles is built up. As the base is extended the triangles get larger and larger, until one of the sides is large enough to become the base of what is called a primary triangle. A system of primary triangles is built up over the whole area, and by this means a number of points on the world's surface are charted. As these points are too far apart for map-making, the primary triangles are broken down into smaller triangles, and thus many new points are fixed.

Obviously it is necessary that each point of any triangle should be clearly visible from each of the other two points, and so in flat country towers have to be erected on the triangulation points chosen. The picture on page 107 shows one of these towers, and it will be seen that it actually consists of two structures, one inside the other. The surveyor's instrument is placed on top of the inner tower, while the outer tower supports a platform round it. In this way the observer can work without causing the tower supporting the instrument to shake.

By permission of]   *[The Director-General, Ordnance Survey.*

A scene in the drawing office.

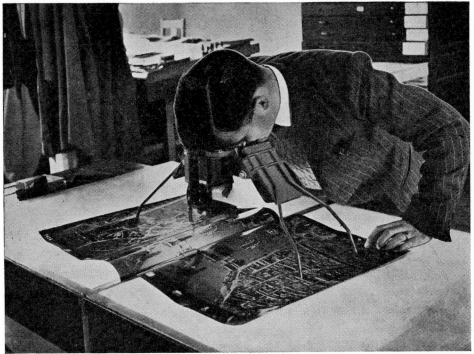

Examining a pair of overlapping air photographs through a stereoscope.

Triangulation, as it is called, is necessary for every survey. The actual making of the map on the ground, which follows this, may be done with the aid of an instrument known as a Plane Table. This may be described as a drawing-board mounted horizontally on a tripod stand and provided with a flat ruler with sights called an alidade. The plane table is set up at a determined point, the position of which is represented by a mark on the paper. The alidade is then set so that by looking through the sights one sees a prominent landmark which it is desired to put on the map and a line is then drawn, with the aid of the alidade, towards this landmark from the point on which one stands. From this same spot several similar observations are taken and then the plane table is moved to another determined position and a further set of observations is taken from there. Eventually the paper will be covered with a maze of fine lines which, however, serve the same purpose as the triangulation —they determine the position of the most important points on the map. Points of detail near any of these fixed points can be determined by measuring with a chain or tape or by pacing.

HOW MAPS ARE MADE

In built-up areas or wooded country the Plane Table is unsuitable, and here the detail is put in by traversing—that is, measuring a series of angles and distances—between known points. This may be done with a compass or, for very accurate work, with an instrument known as a theodolite.

Nowadays aerial photography is widely used in map-making. However, this does not replace triangulation. Points have to be fixed on the ground by triangulation in order to control the aerial photographs. A recent development in survey work from the air is the use of the wonderful invention of radar.

Of course, the lines and triangles do not appear on the finished map; they are merely the framework over which the real map is drawn. Nor will you find much evidence of the triangles on the ground. Near Hounslow and in other parts of Britain you may find monuments marking important bases, and here and there are beacons and cairns; but surveyors, when convenient, use existing landmarks such as church towers. One does find, however, quite a number of

By permission of]   [The Director-General, Ordnance Survey.
Measuring the base with a special " invar " tape.

One of the triangulation towers used in flat country.

bench marks, which are also made by the Ordnance Surveyors. A bench mark takes the form of an upturned arrow with a horizontal line across the point, and it is used in calculating the height of any particular point above sea-level. What may be called the "official" sea-level for Great Britain is marked by the Ordnance Datum in Newlyn Harbour, near Penzance. If you see a hill marked on a map as 360 feet above the sea, you will know "the sea" means the water in Newlyn Harbour at a height which represents the mean sea-level there, as observed over a period of six years.

As may be imagined, the observation and calculation of heights of land above sea-level is extremely laborious, involving the observation of many thousands of points with the aid of highly accurate instruments. Heights above the sea are indicated on maps by isolated figures known as " spot heights." Lines run through series of heights of equal value and form loops known as contours. Like the equator, a contour is an imaginary line, but however hilly the country, if you were to walk along the path of a contour line as shown on the map you would have practically a level path. Contours are drawn at regular intervals of elevation, varying according to the scale of the map. Owing to the slight variation of level, contours hardly appear on maps of flat country like the Lincoln Fens, but in mountainous districts like Wales, Scotland and the English Lake District, the contours are very prominent, and with a little practice one can learn to read from them the approximate shape of a mountain or hill-range. Where the ground rises or falls steeply, for example, the contours will be close together on the map—in the case of

By permission of]   [*The Director-General, Ordnance Survey.*
An air photo mosaic of a built-up area.

a precipice they will actually coincide ; but where the ground slopes more easily, the contours will be well spaced.

After the field work, the map goes to a draughtsman, who makes a fair drawing. This is photographed, and a number of blue bases are printed from the negative. Blue is chosen because it does not photograph. The number of blue bases required depends upon the number of colours to be used in the final map. For a four-colour map, for example, four bases will be made ; and on each will be drawn in the detail that is to be printed in one particular colour. Each of these is photographed, and from the four negatives four separate zinc plates are made. The maps you buy are printed from these plates.

A very important feature of a map is its scale. In Britain we generally speak of map-scales in terms of miles to the inch. On what is called the " half-inch " map, milestones are shown half an inch apart, and on a ten-mile to the inch map, such as motorists use, they would be just a tenth of an inch apart. The more scientific way of referring to scales, however, is by means of Representative Fractions. A scale of $\frac{1}{63360}$ is the " one-inch " map, as you will realise when you remember that there are 63,360 inches in a mile.

WHY WE STREAMLINE CARS, AEROPLANES AND SHIPS

IF you take a large piece of wood and whirl it in the air, you will find that when you have the largest surface to the front, considerable strength is required to move it, while if the narrow edge is forward, the wood seems to " cut " easily through the air. Because air is invisible, we are apt to forget sometimes that it has weight and that, therefore, when " pushed against," it offers resistance. The amount of this resistance depends not only upon the speed, but also upon the size of the surface.

It is easier to appreciate streamlining in water. When the breast stroke is used in swimming the whole chest is offered against the water, and the resistance is much greater than when the side stroke is used to cut through the water. Modern ships not only have sharp knife-like bows, but also smoothly-rounded sides so that the water slides by, instead of striking the sides of the vessel. A bulbous fish-like shape has been proved by tests to be the most efficient.

Air acts very much like water, and that is why we " streamline "

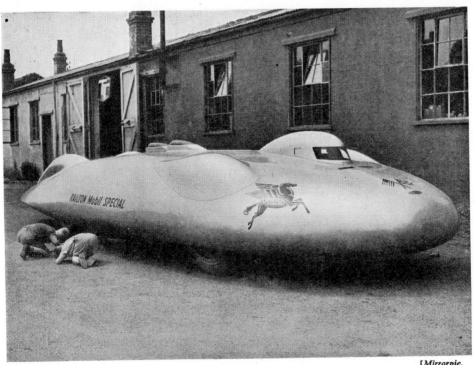

[*Mirrorpic.*

A streamlined racing car.

109

WHY WE STREAMLINE CARS

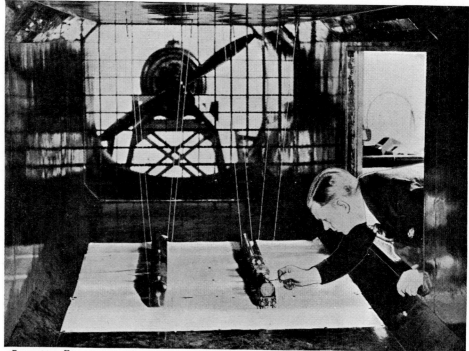

A wind tunnel used to test the effects of streamlining on trains.

our locomotives and cars. Streamlining is not, as so often imagined, merely a question of shaping cars and locomotives so that they cut the air. Indeed, you may notice that the latest streamlined vehicles have rather blunt noses. But you will also see that they are made up entirely of fine curves, that nothing projects, but everything is designed to let the air flow quietly. Put in another way, the less you disturb the air, the less resistance it will offer. You have to move the air when you go through it, but the amount you move it depends very much on your shape, and a correct streamline shape can be defined as the shape which moves the air as little as possible.

Even human beings are slightly streamlined. Our hair is brushed back, our ears lie against our heads. But, of course, streamlining does not matter very much to human beings, because we do not move through the air very quickly. Even in running we do not notice the wind resistance, as we call it, very greatly. It is only when higher speeds are reached that this resistance becomes appreciable, and it is because of the ever-increasing speed of transport that streamlining has become so vitally important.

WHY WE STREAMLINE CARS

Wind resistance increases as the square of the speed. In other words if we need 1,000 horse power to pull a certain vehicle at 10 miles an hour, we shall need 25,000 horse-power to pull it at 50 m.p.h. Nearly all this extra energy is taken up by overcoming the increased resistance of the air. In an actual test it was found when a train was travelling at 40 m.p.h. half the energy was required to conquer wind resistance, the remainder being needed to overcome gravity and friction. When the train accelerated to 80 m.p.h., three-quarters of the energy was taken up by air resistance.

It is fairly obvious that when we set out in our motor car or train, much of our petrol or coal is used in overcoming the air. The question of offering as little resistance as possible is now considered to be one of the first essentials in the search for economy.

Most of the early ideas of streamlined shape were obtained from birds and sea animals. The first stage is to remove everything that

[*Central Press.*

The tank at the National Physical Laboratory, Teddington, in which model ships are tested.

juts out from the main form. This is well illustrated by a comparison between the shape of a modern car and that of the 1910 type. Modern lines are " clean." The lamps do not jut out to offer resistance to the air, but form a curve with the mud-guards. The spare wheel is tucked away. The bonnet is rounded so that the air is able to slip past instead of being brutally pushed aside. It is the same with the streamlined train. Nothing is allowed to project. The sides are perfectly smooth and all whistles, pipes and accessories are completely encased. Even if the whole vehicle has to be made larger, there is far less resistance with a streamlined shape.

An excellent example occurs in the case of aeroplanes, which used to have their landing wheels in " spats." The streamlined casings were bigger than the actual wheels, but their resistance very much less owing to the careful streamlining of every part. Quite small surfaces are important. Racing motor-cyclists have used streamlined helmets, and lamps were sometimes reversed when not wanted so that there was no flat surface to confront the atmosphere. Wheel spokes, too, can mean a reduction of speed.

[Dorien Leigh.

A streamlined motor ferry.

THE HEAD OF AN OIL WELL

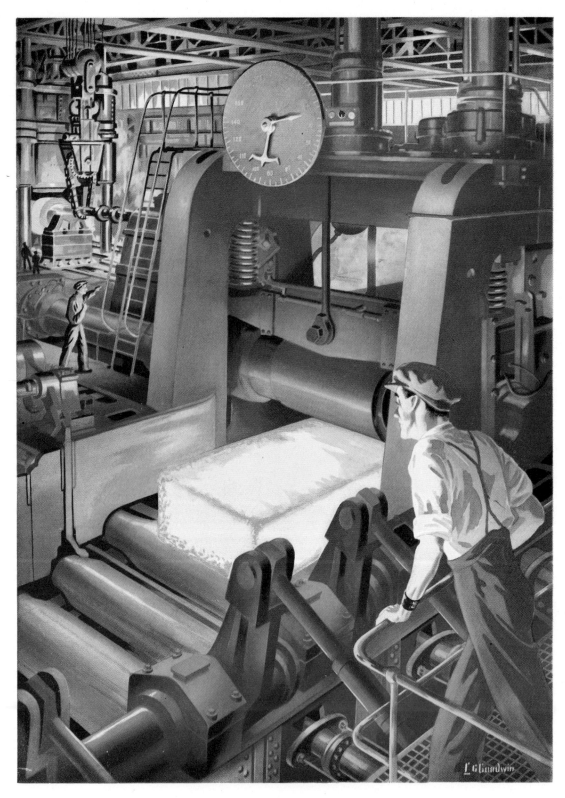

ROLLING WHITE-HOT STEEL

A very fine example of modern motor car design is this experimental Fiat jet car. Months of research into streamlining and wind resistance is carried out before a new car body design is finally approved for production.

In the early days of streamlining, nearly all the attention was paid to the front of the vehicle. It was thought that if this was round and smooth, the air would slip past easily. But a little investigation showed that the dragging effect of the air did not end once it had passed the front ; in fact, a great deal of the resistance was from the rear. The partial vacuum created in the rear by a vehicle moving at great speed may cause as much loss of power as a square front and many protuberances. To-day streamlined vehicles have rather a blunt nose and a gradual slope away towards the back. The designer is particularly careful to see that no vacuum or vortices are created by the rush of air. A streamlined car has no vertical surfaces, but tapers to a gradual end ; any vacuum or air disturbance which might be created underneath the car is avoided by smooth, low mudguarding. In streamlined trains, boards are carried down to the rails to encase the wheels and all coaches are jointed together so that turbulence is not set up between each point of coupling.

The wonderful difference between the streamlined vehicle and the ordinary type was shown in the German train "The Flying Hamburger," which was the first of these trains to make a regular journey at an average speed of 90 m.p.h. When this train passed through a station, it was said that a handkerchief held out on the platform did not flutter. Compare this with the swish and the rush created by an ordinary train running through a station at full speed.

Streamlining is much less important at speeds below 40 m.p.h. and, therefore, it might seem unnecessary to trouble about ordinary touring cars. But we have to remember that the speed of a car through air depends upon the speed of the air as well as that of the car. A vehicle travelling into a moderate wind of 30 m.p.h. at a speed of 40 m.p.h., is moving at 70 m.p.h. relative to the atmosphere, so that streamlining can make an appreciable difference. It may mean ten miles more to the gallon, or expressed in another way, a maximum speed of 60 m.p.h. instead of 50 m.p.h. Then, again, there may be a cross-wind and though streamlining is primarily designed for head-winds, it may reduce the effect of cross-winds to a minimum.

This Avro 707B shows the delta wing design that is a most important development in streamlining aircraft.

By courtesy of]   [*Union-Castle Mail Steamship Co. Ltd.*

The ship's captain at the helm.

HOW A SHIP IS NAVIGATED

THERE must be hundreds of boys who, when on holiday at the seaside, have wondered how the ships which they see passing up and down a few miles away, are navigated from port to port.

In the first place then, for the navigation of a ship certain instruments and books are essential. Chief amongst these are a compass, a sextant, a chronometer (and one may add a patent log), and a nautical almanack for the current year.

In addition, charts of the ports at which the ship is calling are required, and charts of the intervening seas and coasts across and along which the ship has to pass.

Let us take as example, a voyage from Cape Town to Southampton. A glance at a chart of the world makes it evident that the first lap must be to strike across the Atlantic Ocean from Cape Town to the land just south of Cape Verde—the westernmost point of the African continent.

Now a navigator, of course, wants a definite point to steer for— something much less vague than " off the west coast of Africa " ; and

By courtesy of]   [*Union-Castle Mail Steamship Co. Ltd.*

Charting the ship's course in the navigation room.

as a person touring in a car possesses himself of a large-scale map of the part of the country through which he intends to travel, so a sea-farer consults a large-scale chart of the locality for which he is making.

Reference to such a chart of that part of the African coast shows it to be fringed with sunken reefs and shoals quite out of sight of land ; and as the ship will have run over three thousand miles since land was last seen, as a margin of safety one decides to make for a point twenty miles west of the outermost shoal. A calculation, based on trigonometry, is made to find the direction or course to steer to reach this point.

The result thus arrived at is known as the " true course," but is far from what it will be necessary to steer by the ship's compass ; for the mariners' compass is not at all the simple, truthful instrument which most people think it to be. It is quite differently constructed from the pocket compass with which many landsmen are familiar. Instead of the little quivering pointer, in a large brass bowl on a stand, and under a glass cover, is a card showing North and South and the other thirty points of the compass. This card is delicately balanced on a central pivot fitted to the bottom of the bowl, and the secret of its action lies in several small magnetized needles which, invisible from above, are attached to the underside of the card. A vertical line drawn in the exact centre of the inside of the front of the bowl represents the ship's head. When the direction in which the ship is heading is altered, the card, being freely suspended, appears to be turning round inside the bowl, whereas, actually of course, the card is steadily pointing in the same direction, and the bowl and the whole body of the ship is turning round it.

Now for the untruthfulness of the compass. In the first place, a compass needle which points correctly, that is, one which is not dragged by surrounding influences out of the direction in which it naturally lies, points to the Earth's Magnetic Pole, which does not

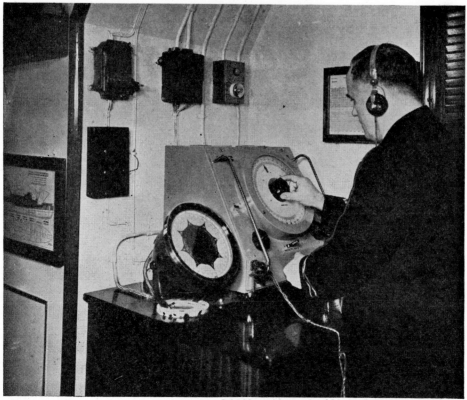

By courtesy of]   *[The Marconi International Marine Communication Co. Ltd.*

The radio officer taking a bearing.

coincide by many miles with the North Pole of the Earth as represented on a map. The angle between these two directions is known as the "variation of the compass," but, inasmuch as it has been calculated for every part of the world, and the result set down on charts, it is, as far as the navigator is concerned, a simple matter to allow for. The main trouble with which he is confronted lies with the ship herself. We all know how, if we hold a piece of iron or steel such as a knife-blade, near a pocket compass, the needle

By courtesy of]   [The Marconi International Marine Communication Co. Ltd.

Operating a " Lodestone " direction-finder.

will follow the movements of the blade. So, on a much larger scale, is the compass on board affected by the iron and steel used in the construction of the ship herself, or carried by her as cargo.

To reduce this deflection of the needle to a minimum, a ship when she is new, and periodically afterwards, has her compasses " adjusted." That is to say, the " deviation " as this deflection is called, is compensated by magnets and pieces of iron placed in various positions round the compass.

In spite of this, however, there is always some small residual error, which alters according to the direction in which the ship is heading, and alters also with the ship's change of latitude as she proceeds on her voyage. The amount of this error is calculated by observations of heavenly bodies several times a day throughout the voyage.

To return to our starting point, having found this total correction (i.e. the combination of variation and deviation) it is applied to the true course, giving us what is known as " the compass course." The ship's head is pointed in that direction (in nautical parlance, the course is set) and the patent log is streamed. At the end of a line of about two hundred and fifty feet in length, a brass rotator is towed in the sea. The inboard end of this line is attached to a small clock affair, the face of which is marked in miles and hundreds of miles.

The revolutions of the rotator depend on the speed at which it is being pulled through the water, and the revolutions communicated through the log-line, actuate a series of cog-wheels inside the " clock " and through these the hands registering the mileage. This constitutes the patent log.

An improvement on the mariners' compass that is largely in use now is the gyro - compass. Controlled by an electric device with a wheel driven at thousands of revolutions per minute, the North point of this compass is held steadily in position pointing to TRUE NORTH, thus doing away with all the

An officer using the radio locator radar installation.

accumulated errors incidental to the ordinary magnetic compass mentioned above.

In connection with the gyro is frequently a mechanical device for steering the ship —commonly known on board as the " Iron Quartermaster." Directly the smallest deviation takes place from the course which has been set, the rudder is automatically altered by the "Iron Quartermaster " sufficiently to counteract the diversion and bring the ship back to her course. Simultaneously the actual course the ship has

By courtesy of]   [The Marconi International Marine Communication Co. Ltd.

The loop aerial of the ship's direction-finder.

made is registered by a line drawn on a slowly-revolving drum, similar to the line on a self-registering barometer. Experience has shown that even in bad weather when the ship is buffeted about and swung off her course by heavy seas, a better course is made when controlled by the " Iron Quartermaster " than when an experienced quartermaster of real flesh and blood is at the helm ! Practically, the only time the live helmsman is utilized is when navigating narrow channels or entering port where the course is being continually altered.

At noon each day, the course the ship has steered, and the estimated distance she has run are worked up, the result being the ship's position by " dead reckoning." The accepted position of the ship, however, is found by observation.

HOW A SHIP IS NAVIGATED

In the ordinary routine on board ship, an observation for longitude is taken about 8 o'clock in the morning. Each officer takes his own " sight " ; that is to say, he measures by his sextant the angular height of the sun above the horizon, noting at the same instant the time shown by the chronometer. From this " altitude," combined with elements of the sun's position taken from the nautical almanac, the correct time at the ship's position is calculated by principles of spherical trigonometry. The chronometer shows the exact time at Greenwich, and the difference between the ship's time and Greenwich time is the ship's longitude—every four seconds of difference representing one mile. At noon the Officers gather together again, and observations are taken for latitude.

Observations of the sun are again taken in the afternoon ; and in most ships, nowadays, the ship's position is found by observations of the stars taken at daybreak and twilight.

In foggy or cloudy weather, when either the horizon or the heavenly bodies are obscured, the navigator has to fall back on " dead reckoning." It is then that the patent log proves most serviceable, and the sounding machine comes into use.

In the old sailing-ship days the only way of finding out the depth of the sea was by the " lead-line "—a small line of some one hundred and twenty fathoms in

Mast and aerial of the radio beacon equipment at a lighthouse.

length marked off in fathoms and weighted with a heavy lead sinker, which took it down to the sea bottom. The depth of water was then found by actual measurement of the submerged line. This was replaced by the "sounding machine," several varieties of which are still in general use.

The principle of the sounding machine is based on the pressure of the ocean at different depths. To the end of about three hundred fathoms of very strong, fine wire, is attached a fifty-six pound lead sinker. Made fast immediately above the

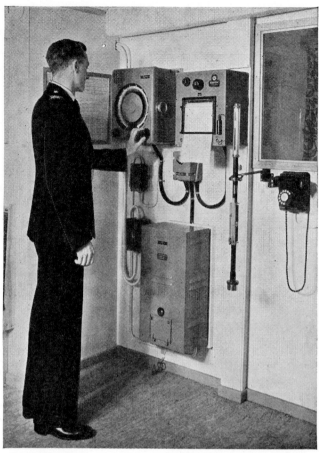

Taking soundings with the echometer equipment.

sinker is a perforated brass tube containing a small glass tube, sealed at the top end, open at the bottom, and coated inside with a coloured preparation of chromate of silver. The wire, which is wound on a revolving drum, is allowed to run out until the lead touches the sea bottom. It is then wound inboard again. The greater the depth to which it—and of course the glass tube with it—has descended, the greater the pressure of the water, and the farther it (the water) has been forced up the prepared tube. Chemical action is set up by the sea-water, and the composition is removed for as far up the tube as the water has been forced. The glass tube is then referred to a graduated scale marked in fathoms ; the depth of water to which the tube has descended being read off from where the red coating ends.

HOW A SHIP IS NAVIGATED

When approaching land in foggy weather, a " cast of the lead "
is taken about every quarter of an hour (perhaps oftener). Should
shoaling water indicate that the ship is approaching too close to the
land, she is at once headed out to seaward.

As the old time " lead-line " was replaced by the sounding
machine, so the latter is now being superseded by electric devices,
the best known of which is perhaps the Echometer. A series of
sounds or impulses is sent out from an electrical instrument in the
chart-room to a connection in the ship's bottom. The sound is
transmitted through the water to the sea-bottom, which sends back
an echo. According to the time that has elapsed between the
sending out of the sound and the return of the echo to the chart-
room, so is the depth of water registered on a marked scale. By
this means, of course, an absolutely continuous line of soundings
can be recorded.

But probably the most valuable of all modern aids to safety

By courtesy of]   [*The Marconi International Marine Communication Co. Ltd.*

A scene in the wireless room, where the radio officer is adjusting the main transmitter.

when approaching land in foggy weather, is given by the adaptation of wireless telegraphy.

On the coasts of most countries frequented by shipping are established what are known as wireless direction finding stations. From these, wireless beams are sent out to seaward, where vessels can pick up the sound, and by means of instruments on board determine the direction from which they come ; or, inversely, if the vessel is not fitted with the special instrument, a series of wireless signals can be sent out from on board, and the shore station will give in reply the vessel's bearing from the station. Where simultaneous bearings of several stations conveniently spaced along the coast can be obtained, an absolute position at the point where the bearings meet each other can be plotted on the chart.

Lighthouses, beacons and buoys are all familiar objects to the seaside visitor, and by marking points of land, the position of dangerous shoals or the fairway of a channel, all add their quota of usefulness to the safe navigation of a ship.

Finally, outside of these brief explanations, there are many details in the guiding of a ship safely to her haven, only to be learned by actual experience, neglect of any of which are liable to lead to wreck and disaster, and all emphasizing the importance of unswervingly acting up to the articles of the Mariners' Creed :— The five L.'s—Latitude, Longitude, the Log, the Lead and the Look-out.

The Creed as most ably expressed by a Mr. Thomas Grey, long since deceased, is as follows :—

I believe in ascertaining the *Latitude* and *Longitude* because it defines my position.

I believe in the *Log* because it checks my distance run.

I believe in the *Lead* because it warns me of dangers invisible to the eye.

I believe in the *Look-out* because it warns me of dangers visible to the eye.

And as I hope to sail my ship in safety on the ocean ; as I wish to spare the lives of my fellow creatures at sea, and as I wish to sail in safety myself all my days, so will I steadfastly practise that in which I believe.

The coins of the English realm.

MINTING MONEY

MOST people have heard of the Royal Mint, the place where money is coined—not *made*. There is a vast difference between *making* money and coining it, though some people, when they hear of others making a lot of money, earning a lot, say they are " coining " it. Only the Royal Mint in this country is allowed to coin money, though at times the Birmingham Mint has coined money under the supervision of Royal Mint officials.

Whence comes the word Mint ? It seems a strange term, probably derived from the latin " Moneta," and the early English word was " mynt." It means a place where coins are produced, and, it is said, the first coins were silver ones made in 269 B.C. in the temple of Moneta in Rome. Hence the term " money " and the derivation " mint."

It may be a surprise to know that money was coined as long ago as 269 B.C., but actually " money " was minted much earlier than that, at least eight hundred years before the coming of Christ, but, of course, coins in those days were very primitive, quite unlike our present ones, or even those made by the Romans, some of which are found from time to time in Great Britain when excavating is going on. They were sometimes in the form of rings, often oddly-shaped ornaments, and sometimes little more than roughly-shaped lumps of metal.

The earliest coins were cast in clay moulds, they were rough in design and finish and usually thick and heavy, especially the copper or bronze ones.

The earliest English mint is said to have existed before the coming of the Romans in 55 B.C. A thousand years ago there were quite a number of mints in various parts of England, and until as recently as 1850, money was minted in England by contractors, many of whom made considerable fortunes. Sir Isaac Newton, when Master of the Mint, discovered how to " make " money, as well as the laws of gravity.

The numerous local mints were gradually closed and from the time of Edward VI all the coinage was concentrated in the Tower. There were only two exceptions, in the period of the Civil War and on the occasion of the great recoinage of 1696 when several local mints were again brought into being. An unauthorised form of coinage, " tokens," used by various business people, was, however, struck by firms in various parts of the country, and occasionally private firms contracted with the Royal Mint to supply coinage —particularly copper and bronze. The present Royal Mint was completed in 1810, and it is here that our money is minted. There are two private firms at Birmingham which undertake the manufacture of colonial and foreign coinages, on behalf of the Royal Mint, London. Coins are no longer cast in moulds as they were in the very earliest days—except those made by counterfeiters— people who are misguided enough to think they can make their own coins and remain undetected. They are now stamped out in huge presses which can produce a million coins a day if required, but let's begin at the beginning.

First the raw material must be obtained, and no matter whether silver or bronze coins are to be made, the raw material delivered to the Mint in " ingots," or small bars, is first " assayed " or analysed and is " alloyed " or mixed with other metals till it has the right composition for the coinage. Years ago when we had gold coins, they were not pure gold ; to 22 parts of gold were added 2 parts of copper, making the standard 22 carats. To-day silver coins are not silver, they would be too soft if they were. From 1920 until 1946, the silver content of each coin was 50 per cent, and the remainder made up of copper, zinc, and nickel, but not to-day.

The Coinage Act, 1946, authorised the substitution of cupro-nickel coins of 75 parts copper, and 25 parts nickel, for all silver coins. All denominations from 2/6 to 6d. issued since January

[Fox Photos Ltd.

Examining newly-made three-penny pieces.

1947 have been struck in this alloy. Bronze coins, pennies, half-pennies and farthings consist nowadays of $95\frac{1}{2}$ per cent. copper, 3 per cent. tin and $1\frac{1}{2}$ per cent. zinc.

When the bars or ingots of metal are correct as regards their composition, the various metals required being alloyed or mixed together in a melting pot or crucible made of plumbago, they are rolled into long strips by being passed through big steel rolls, rather like a glorified washing mangle. Next the thickness of the metal is carefully checked and if it is not the exact thickness required, it must all go back to the melting pot again, but this seldom occurs.

Now the long strips are taken to a " blanking " press, which blanks out flat discs at the rate of one hundred and fifty to eight hundred per minute, leaving very little metal in the strip between blanks. The strip with blanks cut out of it goes back to the melting pot or crucible. Meanwhile the discs or blanks punched out are passed to a machine which thickens the edges.

Next the blanks have to be annealed or softened by being heated in a furnace. They are conveyed continuously through the furnace at such a speed that they attain just the required temperature and then they pass out, comparatively soft and pliable, ready to go to the coining presses. The coining press is very similar to the blanking press, but instead of the blanks being cut by a punch, they are squeezed very hard between two dies, or moulds you might call them, and this causes the metal, though not molten, to " flow " into the design cut, in reverse, in the dies. If the edge is to be " milled " or serrated as in the case of a two-shilling piece, a collar surrounds the blank before pressure is applied to it. This collar has the serrations cut in it and as the dies are forced together on the blank, some of its metal is forced into the serrations around its edge. This coining process hardens the discs again. Now the coin is almost finished, the presses can turn out close on one hundred and twenty coins a minute, keeping pace with the blanking machines, and a battery of twenty machines can turn out close on a million coins a day. Wouldn't it be glorious to be able to stand by even a single machine for a few hours and have all the coins it " coined " during that time, even if they were only shillings !

After being " coined," the coins when made, are very carefully weighed and examined, weighing being carried out by automatic machines which reject any which are not exactly right.

Finally, the coins are counted, again automatically by machinery, and put up in bags for dispatch to the banks and from there they eventually reach you and me, though perhaps never as many of them as we should like, though possibly as many as are good for us. How long do you think coins last? Well, gold sovereigns and half-sovereigns used to last between twenty-five and thirty years in the case of sovereigns and fifteen to twenty years, half-sovereigns. As gold coins in circulation were received at the bank, they were weighed, and if below a certain weight, they were melted down. Milled edges on our silver coins come from the days when our gold coins were milled to prevent people cutting bits of gold off round the edge. Silver coins last from thirty to seventy years. As for copper coins, I have just found in my pocket a penny which is dated 1815 ; it is very battered and if ever it finds its way to the Mint again, it will un-

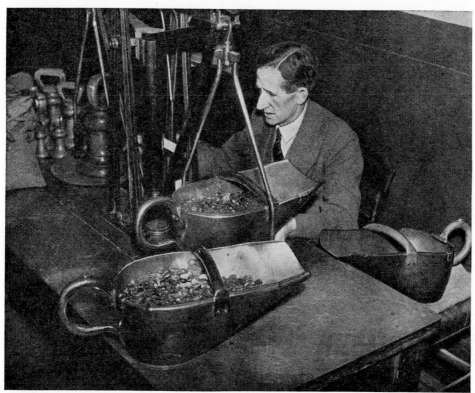

This coin weighing machine is so accurate it will turn if a hair is placed on the scale.

doubtedly be melted down. Another penny is dated 1884 and is in quite good condition. A five-shilling piece which I have carried as a mascot for sixteen years, is in splendid condition, though made in 1896, and St. George is putting up a splendid fight with the dragon. Have you ever seen a crown piece, or a golden sovereign? Lots of young people never have. Perhaps, one day gold coinage will be restored. The Mint could soon turn out all we want if it had the necessary gold. Paper substitutes are useful, but there's something nice about metal money.

By courtesy of]   [Batchelor's Peas Ltd. and E. R. Mottershaw.

Peas being sorted by an electric eye machine.

Aerial view of a petroleum refinery.

PETROL FOR OUR MOTOR CARS

IF we wanted to know the full history of the petrol which drives our cars, we should have to go back many millions of years, watch minute sea creatures moving in oceans where there is now land, imagine their dead bodies falling to the ocean floor and in the course of long ages being fossilised inside rocks. Finally we should have to imagine these rocks being greatly compressed and strongly heated, so that out of the fossilised bodies of these little creatures crude petroleum was slowly formed. Something like this can be done by scientists in their laboratories—and it is the true story of what has happened.

Oil, however, must not merely be formed in the earth, but must be accessible to engineers. Sometimes oil can be profitably extracted from obviously oily shale ; but the great bulk of the world's oil comes from natural reservoirs, which have only to be opened up to release the oil. These reservoirs are contained in " traps " of impervious rocks through which oil cannot pass. Within the traps, if they indeed conceal oil, are porous rocks which are literally soaked in oil, and mixed with the rock and oil is natural gas which, like coal gas, can be used for lighting and heating. As this gas is always stored under pressure, it is only necessary to make a hole through the more solid rock above, and the oil will promptly spout to the surface.

How are these useful rock formations discovered ? In the old days it was largely a matter of trial and error. Oil might be seen at the surface, or someone who had had past experience of oil pro-

By courtesy of]　　　　　　　　　　　　　　　　　[*Shell Photographic Unit.*
Automatic well-drilling machinery.

duction might have a " hunch " that this was " oil country." But nowadays things are very different. Geologists are employed to seek likely rock formations in distant parts of the world ; and experts known as " geophysicists " are brought along to try to discover, with their instruments, where oil-bearing formations may be expected to be found.

One method which geophysicists use is to make artificial earth-quakes, by blowing up a charge of explosive. They were led to this rather strange procedure by the facts, which earthquake experts had

A modern oil tanker.

been able to discover, from real earthquakes, about the inside of the earth. The secret in this case is that " earth waves," from the miniature earthquake, are reflected from the top of the oil " trap " —if there is one. Moreover, by timing how long it is before the reflected wave comes back to the surface, it is possible to calculate how deep the buried trap may be. Another method makes use of a very delicate instrument known as a " torsion balance." This

Laying pipe lines.

measures variations in the gravitational pull of the rocks beneath.

However, all that the geophysicist and geologist can do is to tell the engineers whereabouts they think drilling should be carried out. They cannot be sure that there is really oil beneath, however promising the arrangement of the rocks may appear. So the next step is to bore a well and see.

Modern oil wells are bored by a rotating cutter, which literally eats its way into the rock, the well being automatically provided with a metal lining as fast as it is bored. But, although these machines are wonderfully efficient, oil boring may be an expensive business. Anything up to £100,000, or even more, may be invested

By *courtesy of*]   [*Shell Photographic Unit.*

Drilling for crude oil in Queensland, Australia.

on sinking a new well—and at the end of it all there may be no oil to tap. There is a well in California which is 8,201 feet deep, which has never produced a drop of oil. This is nearly twice as deep as the tallest mountain in the British Isles is high.

Then, if the engineers are lucky, they will be greeted with a great spout of oil, welling up through the trap which they have pierced, and many thousands, even millions, of gallons of oil may run to waste in the first rush unless suitably controlled by strong well-head fittings. For some time, depending on the pressure below, the oil will go on shooting up to the surface without any further effort. But, in the end, the pressure will always drop as the natural reservoir is depleted, and pumping machinery must be installed if the well is to be kept working. Most oil wells are worked in this way, although the newer wells which flow naturally produce a larger amount of oil in proportion. Owing to this need for pumping, the average output of the American oil fields, which still produce nearly half the world's oil, is no more than about a ton and a half a day from each well.

From the oil fields the oil is conveyed in pipelines to a refinery or to the nearest convenient harbours for shipment and refining overseas. It is cheaper to carry oil by pipeline than by rail. The United States alone has about 139,000 miles of oil pipe-lines, and a further 25,000 miles of lines used to convey natural gas. But the most ambitious pipe-lines of all are those linking the Iraq oil fields, north of Baghdad, with the Mediterranean ports of Haifa and Tripoli, near Damascus. These lines cross the rivers Tigris and Euphrates, as well as hundreds of miles of desert. Together, they are 1,120 miles long and cost £9,250,000 to lay.

Crude petroleum is of no use by itself and it is the business of the oil refineries to split it up into the products used in everyday life, such as petrol, kerosene, fuel, bitumen, etc. This is done by heating the crude oil to a temperature which will permit the more volatile parts to be distilled off in the form of separate products. One of the most volatile parts is petrol and after that kerosene, which is used as lamp oil, fuel oil and so on. In addition, further supplies of petrol can be produced by a process known as " cracking." This means that some of the heavier, and chemically more compli-cated, parts of the crude oil can be split up or " cracked," forming lighter and less complicated parts, such as " petrol."

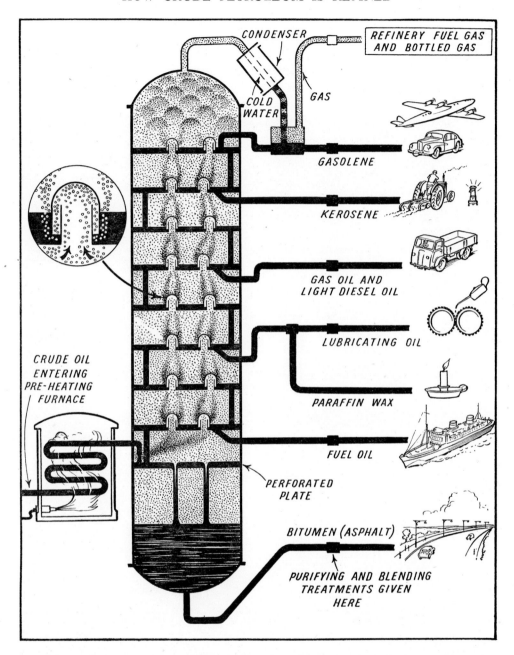

CONDENSER

REFINERY FUEL GAS AND BOTTLED GAS

COLD WATER

GAS

GASOLENE

KEROSENE

GAS OIL AND LIGHT DIESEL OIL

LUBRICATING OIL

PARAFFIN WAX

FUEL OIL

CRUDE OIL ENTERING PRE-HEATING FURNACE

PERFORATED PLATE

BITUMEN (ASPHALT)

PURIFYING AND BLENDING TREATMENTS GIVEN HERE

Finally, the petrol produced by the refineries is fed through more pipes into tankers, ships which are no more than floating oil tanks, and carried to us in this country. Other tankers carry crude petroleum to be refined at English ports instead of at its country of origin, for it is not necessary to refine the oil before shipment. Add to all this the fleets of petrol-tank lorries which carry petrol to every village in the country, and the ingenious working of a petrol pump, and it will be realised that the feeding of our motor cars is a complicated business.

Filling a 40-gallon oil drum.

Rolling a bar of stainless steel.

STAINLESS STEEL

R USTY knives being such an obvious nuisance, one might have imagined that some chemist deliberately set to work to produce a steel that would not rust, and that stainless steel was the result. Nothing of the sort happened. The discovery of stainless steel was a pure accident and it came about like this. In 1912, a metallurgist, that is an expert in metals, Mr. Harry Brearley, was studying wear in rifle barrels with the patriotic object of finding a steel which would wear better than the ones then in use. Among many others, he made a small sample of a steel containing a larger proportion of the metal chromium than either he or anyone else had ever tried before. Like many others of his sample steels, it was put through a routine series of mechanical tests, and found wanting. Also like many others, the broken pieces from the tests were thrown into a corner of Mr. Brearley's laboratory and forgotten. The difference was that a fortnight later Mr. Brearley's assistant happened to notice that these pieces of steel, alone of the pile of rejects, had not rusted. Mr. Brearley was interested, and without saying anything about it, had a knife forged from the pieces. He took it home, and put it out in his garden for a month, so as to give rain and air the best

139

possible chance to rust it. At the end of this time the knife was still bright—the first stainless knife, and a much more important discovery to the world at large than any improvement he could possibly have brought about in rifle barrels.

This story, whatever its moral may be, shows one very important fact about iron—which is that the addition of other chemical elements to it has very important effects on the way it behaves. Steel is, in fact, only iron to which other elements have been added in precisely-controlled proportions and under the right conditions.

If we want to see why it is necessary to make steel at all, we have only to look in turn at " cast iron," and at " wrought iron," to discover that neither is altogether satisfactory. " Cast iron " is iron as it is originally made in a blast furnace from its ores. Coke, which mainly consists of carbon, is used in the furnaces, and so cast iron contains anything from 1.5 to 4.5 per cent. of carbon which it has picked from the coke. The effect of the carbon is to make the iron very hard and very brittle. It is, therefore, of very limited use for constructional work, or indeed for any purpose in which it will have to withstand sudden strains. Probably, any schoolboy has seen an iron-legged desk which has had its legs broken. They would not have broken if they had been made, more expensively, of steel. On the other hand " wrought iron " which is very nearly pure iron, though strong, is relatively soft. Iron nails are made of it, and one knows how easily they can be bent in the course of hammering. What is wanted, therefore, is a form of iron which is both hard and strong—that is, steel.

The simplest and oldest way of making steel is to heat bars of the purest possible wrought iron for a week or so in a small furnace packed with charcoal at a temperature well below the melting point of the iron. A small amount of carbon is absorbed from the charcoal, enough to make the iron hard, but very much less than there is in " pig iron." A very pure steel is produced in this way, but it is obvious that the method is not one which is suited to large-scale production, and success is entirely dependent on skilled judgment on the part of the workers. However, this process does illustrate what are the essentials in steel making—namely to produce iron which is either nearly pure, or at least contains a known and low content of carbon, and then to add whatever else is wanted to it. In the two chief commercial processes, the Bessemer and the " open hearth "

By courtesy of]   [Firth-Vickers Stainless Steels Ltd.

Rolling sheets of stainless steel.

processes, the iron is in each case molten. This is necessary for the removal of unwanted impurities, and at the same time speeds-up the addition of what more is wanted.

Quite a large number of different chemical elements are added to iron to produce the different steels required by commerce, and even to-day it is safe to say that only a small proportion of the possible useful steels have yet been made. Manganese, chiefly familiar in the form of the purple disinfectant " permanganate," is one ; and silicon most commonly found in sand, another. Chromium, as the essential constituent of stainless steel, has already been mentioned. Nickel, which like chromium is used in plating, is another useful addition to steel, and so is cobalt, which is a near chemical relation of nickel. Tungsten and molybdenum are other metals which often find their way into steels, and there are many others which might be used. Remembering that the proportions in which these elements are added are important, that the addition of a second element may modify the effects of the first, and that the conditions of manufacture need to be precisely controlled, it is easy to see that the making of steel is a life study in itself.

The exact control of conditions being a matter of importance, many of the special steels needed by modern industry are made in electric furnaces. This is the case with stainless steel. Steel scrap, odd-shaped and comparatively worthless pieces from other parts of the works, is charged through a door into the furnace. If it is an arc furnace (more than one type of electric furnace may be used), three carbon electrodes will be sticking through the roof. If you take an ordinary flashlight battery and, holding a piece of carbon rod against each terminal, touch them almost together, you will obtain a very small arc. This is the principle on which the furnace works, only on a much larger scale. An arc furnace, such as is used in making stainless steel, may take as much current as a hundred thousand ordinary electric lamps. The intense heat of the arc melts the steel in two to three hours.

Stainless steel, in the strict and original sense of the word, consists of steel containing from 9-16 per cent. of chromium and not more than .7 per cent. of carbon. That is the formula which Mr. Brearley discovered when trying to improve the wear of rifle barrels. But there are all manner of different steels, designed to resist corrosion, whether by the air and water or by acids, so that it is now possible

By courtesy of]   [Firth-Vickers Stainless Steels Ltd.

Removing liquid stainless steel from a 30-ton electric furnace.

to produce a steel which will stand up to almost any conditions.

If the amount of chromium is raised to 18 per cent., and 2 per cent. of nickel is also added, a special type of stainless steel is produced which is largely used for many of the machined fittings on aeroplanes. Yet another type of stainless steel contains the same amount of chromium, 18 per cent., but as much as 8 per cent. of nickel. This is both strongly acid-resisting and has a great capacity for being stretched without breaking. Even strong nitric acid can be handled in storage and transport tanks made of this steel. Dye-vats and milk tanks are also often made of it, and it is frequently used in the frameworks of aeroplanes, and for restaurant fittings and in modern furniture. Finally, other types of steels, containing up to 25 per cent. of chromium, together with 6 to 25 per cent. of nickel, are used to provide strength at high temperatures, for example in furnace parts. And, in still other steels, silicon is used as well as chromium. The uses of all these steels are very varied, but the stainless steel table-knife is still, probably, the greatest monument of Mr. Brearley's original discovery.

[B.O.A.C.

Stainless steel is used in the construction of the framework of this giant airliner.

Cross-pollinating an orchid.

HUNTING FOR RARE PLANTS

THERE are flowers that are worth fortunes. The most costly and prized of all are the rare varieties of orchids. There is a peculiar fascination about orchids. Collectors are willing to pay almost any sum to obtain a rare type. Not long ago a man bought an orchid for £75. He was a shrewd gentleman. He showed it to some wealthy collectors. They were eager to buy it from him. Eventually, he divided it into eight parts, and sold each part for £250, making a profit altogether of £1,925 on the plant.

It is in the hot, damp and remote tropical jungles that orchids are found. To obtain them men must face all manner of dangers and problems. Plant-hunting is by no means a profession for the nervous person or the weakling.

There are many flowers far more common than orchids, which we should never have seen in our gardens had it not been for the plant-hunters. The tulip, crocus and iris come from Persia and Kurdistan; daffodils and carnations come from Asia Minor; cosmos, nasturtiums and dahlias come from Mexico, and roses come from India and China. In fact, there seems to be scarcely a

This unusual looking plant is a rare and valuable orchid.

country in the world that has not contributed towards the beauty of English flower gardens.

All these flowers had to be searched for. Before they could obtain the plants they sought, men had to climb mighty mountains, cross bleak plateaux, fight their way through fever - ridden jungles, hack a path through bamboo forests, and win the friendship of suspicious natives.

An orchid - hunter, after tracking down a rare specimen in the depths of the jungle, discovered that the plant was looked upon as sacred by the native tribe who lived in the territory. He won their friendship but was told that only men of royal blood were permitted to handle the flower. They explained to him that if he would marry the chief's daughter, he would then be of royal blood, and could have the flower. Undaunted, the plant-hunter agreed. As soon as the marriage ceremony was over he packed the plant, and, without waiting to say good-bye to his jungle bride, started hot-foot for home !

An interesting experience of a different kind befell Captain Kingdon-Ward, most famous of all modern plant-hunters. Captain Kingdon-Ward has made many expeditions to various remote parts of Asia, and discovered the wonderful Blue Poppy growing at a height of seven thousand feet on the Tibet-Burma frontier. He, like other plant-hunters, has to be an expert on many subjects besides botany. He has to know many languages. He must know how to fend for himself, because he is out of touch with civilization for months at a time. Perhaps most important of all, he needs to know quite a lot about medicine and first-aid. At any time he may get poisoned, bitten or hurt ; he is almost sure to fall a prey to some kind of fever, he may have an accident and break a limb, and he must know how to doctor himself, because there is no one else to do it for him.

This knowledge of medicine was useful to Captain Kingdon-Ward on one occasion. He had crossed the frontier of Tibet, and was in territory forbidden to Europeans. He went to the Lama's monastery to ask permission to search for new flowers, but doubted whether he would obtain it. On arrival, however, he found the monastery a place of woe. The Lama was ill. He asked for Kingdon-Ward, and commanded the explorer to cure him. This Kingdon-Ward was able to do, for his knowledge of medicine told him that the Lama's illness was only of a slight nature, and he was

able to prepare some pills which cured the sick man. As a reward for this service, the Lama gave him permission to stay in the district as long as he wished, to search where he liked, and to take away any plants that he fancied. The result was that Kingdon-Ward was able to return home bringing specimens of flowers which no Englishman had ever seen before.

The plant-hunter's troubles are not over when he has obtained his specimens. He is faced with the task of getting them all the way back home, and getting

Lovely—and costly !

them back alive. Captain Kingdon-Ward carries most of his specimens in vacuum flasks to preserve them against changes of temperature. Some people prefer air-tight tin boxes. Quite a number
of plant-hunters are now making frequent use of the air mail in
order to rush their finds back to England at the best possible speed,
but there are still plenty of places in Asia which are about a
month's journey from an aerodrome.

When a plant-hunter goes off on an expedition, he generally
expects to be away for a year or eighteen months. This means
carrying a lot of stores and equipment, and makes it necessary for
him to engage a team of native porters. These natives can be a
source of great trouble and annoyance, even though by the time the
trip is over the plant-hunter has taught them how to handle his
specimens. On one such trip a hunter was fortunate to get hold of
a particularly intelligent head-boy. They hadn't been many days
out when the head-boy brought him a rare plant that he had found.
The collector was delighted, and rewarded him with a present.
The next day his tent was besieged by the rest of the porters, all

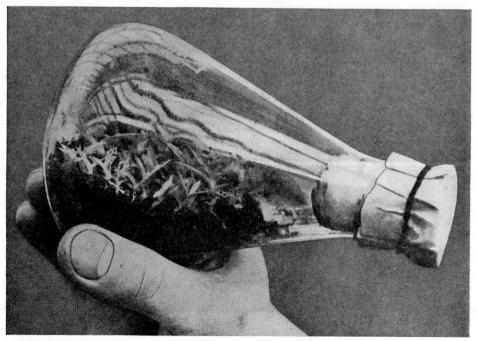

ORCHIDS IN PHIALS
Great care is needed during the early stages of the cultivation of rare orchids.

Rearing young orchids in pans.

bringing quite common plants that they had rooted up. Of course, none of them were any use to the collector, but the natives were too dull to understand why one plant should be valuable and another worthless. For days they continued to bring in useless specimens, in the hope of getting some payment, and when no reward was forthcoming, they turned sullen and sulky, a number of them deserted, and the collector was forced to curtail his expedition and return to his base.

On another expedition some porters asked permission to make a pet of a wild goat. The collector readily agreed, providing they looked after the animal. All went well until the return journey. The collector was feeling pleased with himself. Twelve months' arduous work had resulted in well-filled specimen boxes. One day, when they had pitched camp, the collector spread out some rubber ground-sheets, and laid out his seeds and other specimens, to dry them in the sun. He retired to his tent to write up some reports. Some time later he heard a peculiar munching sound. Filled with a terrible foreboding, he rushed from the tent. His worst fears were confirmed. The pet goat was standing in the middle of the ground-sheet, wagging its jaws contentedly. The beast had made a clean sweep of a whole year's work by eating all the specimens.

This drawing of these strange fish of the deep is based on drawings made on one of Dr. Beebe's expeditions. 1. A Viper Fish. 2. A Great Gulper Eel. 3. Three-star Angler Fish. 4. A Serpent Dragon. 5. A Pipe Fish. 6. Illuminated Constellation Fish. 7. A shoal of Scarlet Arrow Worms. 8. A Black Swallower with (10) its meal inside it. 9. A Scarlet Shrimp repelling a Dragon Fish (11). 12. A Deep-sea Squid. 13. Deep-sea Sailfins.

EXPLORING THE OCEAN DEPTHS

FAR beneath the surface of the sea, where it is too deep for even the faintest gleam of sunlight to penetrate, there exists in utter darkness a nightmare world swarming with strange creatures utterly unlike any you have ever seen.

The inhabitants of the ocean depths range from tiny beings as thin as paper and as transparent as glass to hideous grey-coloured monsters over twenty feet in length.

Until a few years ago, the only way in which naturalists could obtain specimens of these deep-water creatures was by lowering a trawl-net from a boat, and then hoisting it up again in the hope that an interesting catch had been made.

Specimens obtained in this way were always dead by the time they were brought to the surface, and often were found to be mangled and shapeless, so that it was almost impossible to imagine what they looked like when they were alive. The reason for this was that they lived hundreds of feet below the sea, where the weight of water pressing on their bodies was so enormous that human beings would be crushed to pulp, and Nature had provided these creatures with bodies that would withstand the pressure. But as soon as they were drawn up into shallower waters, where the weight was less, the pressure inside their bodies was greater than the pressure outside. As a result many of them burst, or were mangled.

The only sea creatures which could be watched in their native haunts were the ones that live in shallow water, where they could be reached by a man wearing a diving helmet, or viewed through the floor of a glass-bottomed boat.

One of the finest places in the world for viewing sea creatures in this way is in the water around Nonsuch Island, in the Bermudas. The sea is so clear that one is able to see farther down through it at this spot than anywhere else on earth. Because of this, it has always been a favourite place of naturalists interested in marine life, and especially of Dr. William Beebe.

Time after time Dr. Beebe went down, wearing only a diving helmet. Ten fathoms was about as deep as he dared go, but often he would walk out to the edge of a steep under-sea precipice, and peer longingly into the fathomless blue-black gulf beneath him, trying to imagine what the inhabitants of that unreachable place looked like, and wishing with all his heart that he could find some method of getting down there.

151

EXPLORING THE OCEAN DEPTHS

Dr. Beebe's wish was granted.

A friend of his, Mr. Otis Barton, invented an astonishing metal diving chamber, called a Bathysphere.

The globe is five feet in diameter. There is just room for two men to cramp themselves into it. It has windows made of fused quartz, the strongest and most transparent substance on earth. The windows are three inches in thickness. It is fitted with a tank containing forty gallons of oxygen, a number of scientific instruments, a first-aid kit, apparatus to keep the air pure, and a telephone.

In the Bathysphere Dr. Beebe and Mr. Barton have made a large number of descents into the ocean, going down to depths far greater than any other man has ever attempted.

On their first trip the ocean explorers went down to a depth of eight hundred feet. The sphere was fitted with a powerful search-light to illuminate the dark water, but Dr. Beebe switched it off. The two friends sat side by side, gazing out into blackness. For a while nothing stirred. Then the darkness came alive with a myriad flashing lights. A school of Silver Hatchetfish were approaching the globe. The fish were phosphorescent. Living in darkness, they carried their own illumination. Other fish came, ablaze with shimmering blue, green, orange or red.

Dr. Beebe was at the telephone, to describe what he saw. It had been arranged with the men in the boat from which the Bathysphere was controlled that a silence of five seconds would indicate that the explorers were in trouble.

They listened, but heard no sound of Dr. Beebe's voice. The seconds passed, and they grew more and more anxious, feeling certain that something very serious had happened. But at last he spoke. Everything was all right. He had been so enthralled by all that he had seen, that he had quite forgotten about the men up above who were waiting to hear from him.

Following the success of the first descent, Dr. Beebe and his friend have made many more. On one occasion they went down to a depth of three thousand and twenty-eight feet, well over half a mile. At this depth there was a pressure of more than half a ton of water on every square inch of the sphere, and the quartz windows were holding back a pressure of nineteen tons.

Even so, Dr. Beebe asked to be lowered farther still, but the

THE BATHYSPHERE

In this two-ton sealed ball, deep sea explorers can descend to a depth of over three thousand feet.

captain of the boat refused to take the responsibility. There were only about a dozen turns of cable left on the windlass.

It was a wonderful experience for the two explorers, as they saw the broad fan of their searchlight blazing out through the pitch-black waters, for it was the first light to penetrate that watery darkness since the seas were created. For billions of years darkness had reigned there, and they were the first men to look out on its wonders.

They saw fantastic things.

A great grey shadow loomed, and passed slowly through the beam of light. It was a strange, hitherto unknown denizen of the deep — the biggest creature Dr. Beebe had ever seen. It was illuminated by hundreds of little lights all along its body, all glittering like jewels.

On another occasion, when the searchlight had been switched off, and they were sitting in darkness, the two men were astonished by a sudden burst of light outside the window, which lasted for about six seconds. It seemed to be some kind of under-water explosion.

They were puzzled as to its cause, and waited to see whether it would be repeated. It did occur again, and this time they saw that the flash was being produced by a huge shrimp, to scare off a shoal of fish that were chasing it. The light was the shrimp's weapon of defence. Its vivid glow startled the pursuing shoal and sent the fish scuttling away.

The underwater scene was constantly changing. It was full of movement and drama. They saw a grim battle in which a Finger-squid fought and killed a Lantern-fish. The Squid was typical of the fantastic creatures that inhabit the undersea world. It had two enormous eyes, with luminous white spots on the iris. It was equipped with long arms, deadly suckers, and on the tips of the two longest arms were huge orange lights.

These things and many more Dr. Beebe has seen. But there must certainly be still greater marvels beneath the ocean, which no human being has yet seen. Three-quarters of the globe is covered by sea, and four-fifths of the sea is more than five thousand feet deep. At present all that vast realm is beyond the reach of even the Bathy-sphere, unexplored and unknown.

[*Mirrorpic.*

This ingenious burglar alarm is fitted in a bank and will foil even the most careful robber. From the black circle an invisible beam of infra-red rays is projected into the room which will detect the presence of anyone moving about. Even the beam of a torch is enough to set the alarm bells clanging.

155

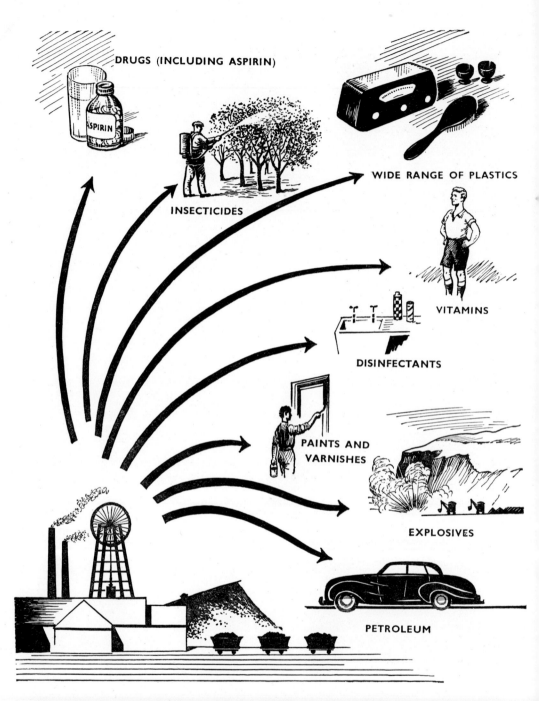

DRUGS (INCLUDING ASPIRIN)

INSECTICIDES

WIDE RANGE OF PLASTICS

VITAMINS

DISINFECTANTS

PAINTS AND VARNISHES

EXPLOSIVES

PETROLEUM

For many years coal was used only for heating people's homes and providing power for industry. Nowadays, all manner of valuable by-products, some of which are shown above, are obtained from the waste that is left over from the manufacture of coke and gas. This waste was long considered useless.

WHAT COAL GIVES US

COAL is this country's most important natural inheritance. Looking at a lump of coal, as it burns on the family fire, it is not at once easy to realise its varied usefulness. Yet coal provides Britain with roughly nine-tenths of its light, heat and industrial power. It gives us coke, gas, steam and electricity. It provides the blast furnaces of this country with their heat and the cotton mills with their power. Coal, moreover, is a vast potential source of chemicals, the chief of which are tar, benzole and ammonia. From tar alone it is possible to build up many more different chemicals than there are stars in the sky which can be counted with the naked eye.

The presence of these by-products in coal is accounted for by the fact that coal, as we all know, comes from the forests and vegetations of millions of years ago, which have fallen to the ground, decayed, and as soil has accumulated fresh forests and vegetations have sprung up. The sun, wind and rain have again had their way, these forests have fallen to the ground and so the process has gone on and on with the added effect of heat and pressure. Thus what we now get from coal as by-products, was originally present in the plants and vegetations of millions of years ago. The means by which these products have been discovered present a fascinating story which would be too long to recount in this article. One or two incidents which illustrate how the discoveries came about are interesting and were, in most instances, the result of hard and intensive research work.

A man named McIntosh discovered that some of the spirit contained in tar had the effect of dissolving rubber into the form of a solution. He coated pieces of fabric with this solution and proved its waterproof qualities. As a result of his discovery, the first mackintosh was made, which name has remained ever since for those waterproof garments.

A man named Lister later found that one of the distillates of tar contained Carbolic, which could be used as a disinfectant in surgical operations, and this was the beginning of antiseptic surgery.

In the middle of the 19th century, a young British chemist named Perkin found that he could obtain synthetically from benzene, aniline dyes similar to the dyes which were obtained from natural organic substances. His discovery really accounted for the foundation of the dye-stuffs industry. These by-products of coal provide the source of practically all modern dye-stuffs, from the most brilliant reds to the most delicate mauves and greens.

Nature, or perhaps we should say Providence, has endowed us poor mortals with these products, as will be seen later in this article. We can use them wisely, in which event they can be used for our creature comforts, our pleasures and alleviation of pain, or we can use them foolishly to destroy one another and inflict pain and destruction everywhere. Toluole is one excellent example of this fact. From toluole we can obtain saccharine, the excellent sweetening agent, or alternatively we can convert that toluole into tri-nitro-toluene (T.N.T., a deadly explosive).

Phenol is another example of this principle, but this important derivative is obtained from carbolic acid on the tar side of the picture. Amongst a multitude of products to be obtained from phenol are picric acid for explosives purposes on the one hand, or wintergreen, phenacetin and salycylic acid for the manufacture of aspirin on the other. But these can also be obtained synthetically as explained later.

Coal, therefore, has two main uses: the obvious one as a fuel and the less obvious one as a chemical storehouse. The steam engine, in any form, gets its power from either coal or oil, and mostly from coal. Electricity, however wonderful in itself, is no more than a convenient way of distributing power, and in this country coal is the first source of most of the power which comes into our homes as electricity. Coal is burnt in furnaces, used to turn water into steam, and the expansive power of the steam is used to drive the dynamos which give us electricity. Out of the two hundred and fifteen million tons of coal used in this country about forty-three million tons are used in the generation of electricity for every kind of use.

A gas main is only another way of conveying coal from place to place. Only, in this case, it is part of the fuel which coal contains which is brought to our houses, and not just power derived from it. We may say that we cook, or heat our rooms by gas or electricity, as the case may be, but it is well to remember that in each case it is the same black lump of coal that we are using—in another form.

If coal is heated with all the air excluded, it does not behave in the same way as it does on the family fire. There, it is true, we can see jets of gas pouring out from cracks in the coal and burning brightly for a short time. Sometimes also we may see something very like tar oozing out on to the surface of the coal, and the cinders from a fire which has been allowed to go out are not very different from the coke which is often used to feed a hot-water boiler in the kitchen. In coke ovens, however, the by-products and gases are extracted

General view of a steel works.

from the coal on a big scale, leaving behind the carbon portion of the coal in the form of coke, which is supplied in this country in enormous quantities to the iron and steel industry and for domestic purposes. When the coal is treated in a gasworks all of the gas is driven off and collected in gas-holders to supply our mains, once again coke being left behind in the retort or oven in which the heating has taken place. That is why coke does not burn so easily as coal. Coke is coal which has lost its most easily inflammable part, as well, for that matter, as the part which burns smokily. So, although coke never smokes, it cannot be used in an open grate, for the draught up the chimney is not strong enough to make it burn.

However, for the benefit of those of us who need smokeless fires, some works treat part of their coal less drastically, and produce, instead of coke, various varieties of what are known as " smokeless fuels ". These are half way between coal and coke. They have had enough of the original coal taken away to prevent them smoking, and enough left to enable them to burn in an open grate.

Now we come to the by-products, the most interesting, although highly complicated process. The three primary by-products which are given off when the coal is used for the production of coke for the iron and steel industry or for the production of gas are tar, benzole and ammonia. The crude tar is distilled and split up into certain fractions. Amongst these fractions is carbolic oil, which contains disinfectants. As mentioned previously, the carbolic oil also can be worked up by a chemical process to produce pure phenol—the most important product in the plastics and explosives industry, and the chief raw material used for making the celebrated bakelite, one of the first plastics ever produced. As the term " plastics " is closely associated with by-products, it may be helpful to explain that the term " plastics " covers modern materials of construction which, in many cases, replace metals, wood and ceramics. They are not mined, as are metals, nor grown, as is wood, but they are the result of a complicated chemical reaction during the course of which they are formed under the action of heat and pressure into the required shape. Another fraction of the oils, viz. naphthalene oil, provides a starting point for antiseptics such as dettol, whilst they also form the basis of plastics and explosives.

Creosote oil is used as a preservative of wood, whilst anthracene oil, the heaviest oil, forms the basis of winter washes for fruit trees. The naphthalene oil contains a residue or paste known as naphthalene ; this naphthalene is used for making dyes, explosives and plastics, and may be taken further into the chemical industry for the manufacture, indirectly, of such products as cellulose acetate (a basis of artificial silk), and its range widens as it extends further into the chemical field where it is used as a food preservative, in the pharmaceutical industry, perfumery trade, paint trade, etc.

When the tar oils have been distilled, a residue, pitch, is left. This is used as a binder for making patent fuels in the form of briquettes and ovoids. A certain grade of pitch is also used in the manufacture of electrodes.

160

Plant for producing Benzole and Ammonia.

During the Second World War pitch was blended with creosote to form creosote-pitch mixture or tar fuel oil, an excellent fuel oil used as a substitute for imported black oil from petroleum. This tar fuel oil is becoming increasingly popular in the steel trade and in industry generally on account of its superior flame luminosity and low sulphur content.

In addition, creosote-pitch mixture is a basis for the direct manufacture of carbon black—a reinforcing material used for the strengthening of the walls of motor tyres.

From tar is also obtained road tar, a material from which many of the excellent roads in this country are made.

Coming next to benzole, coal produces nearly 26 millions gallons of crude benzole per annum, from which is derived motor benzole, a fuel which when blended with petrol gives us a mixture much favoured by motorists. This crude benzole, in addition to the motor benzole, contains a number of most valuable derivatives. The first one on the distillation scale is pure benzole. Pure benzole was used during the war because of its high octane value and other advantages as an aviation spirit. It enabled us to put our very heavy bombers into the air when the normal aviation spirit failed.

Pure benzole also gives us, indirectly, a raw material for aspirin, whilst it is used in the dye-stuffs and explosives industry and forms the basis for the manufacture of pure phenol synthetically, from which we also derive wintergreen, phenacetin, salycylic acid and D.D.T.

The next product obtained is toluole which in addition to providing tri-nitro-toluene and saccharine, is also used for such a wide variety of purposes as the manufacture of gold size used in gold leaf paint ; an inhibitor to prevent the formation of mould in ladies' cosmetics ; the manufacture of dyestuffs, flavours and perfumes and as a food preserver.

Another product from crude benzole is solvent naphtha, a solvent used widely in the rubber industry to dissolve raw rubber. During the war solvent naphtha was used extensively in connection with the manufacture of barrage balloons. It is also used to produce leather substitute or cloth and has innumerable other uses.

Yet a further product is xylole, used very largely as a solvent in the paint trade. It has a wide market in the lacquer and varnish industry, also for furniture and floor polishes. It is also used as a solvent in the manufacture of inks and in the printing trade, particularly for photogravure work or, in other words, colour printing. During the war xylole was used extensively for the manufacture of special dope with which to paint Mosquito aeroplanes.

A very unpleasant but important additional product of the benzole group is pyridine, the most noticeable characteristic of which is its foul smell, which qualifies it for an important market as a denaturent for commercial alcohol. The incorporation of a little pyridine in commercial alcohol deters the more thirsty element from using it as a beverage. Pyridine, also, is used to produce that wonderful drug M & B. It is used as a wetting agent for textiles and in photographic chemicals.

It is possible to obtain petrol from coal direct by the hydrogenation process. Although it was the intention of Imperial Chemicals Industries, Ltd. originally to hydrogenate coal on a big scale, which process involved the heating of coal under pressure with hydrogen, it was found that creosote oil lent itself much more readily to the hydrogenation process, and I.C.I. have now been hydrogenating creosote for a number of years past with complete success.

WHAT COAL GIVES US

Coming finally to the third raw material, ammonia liquor, we once again get the illustration of war use or peacetime use for our by-products. Ammonia liquor can form the basis of ammonium nitrate and ammonal, two deadly explosives. Alternatively, the ammonia liquor can be manufactured into sulphate of ammonia, a fertilizer used to improve crop production by our agricultural industry. Again, ammonia liquor can also be concentrated into pure ammonia liquor, when it is used for the production of soda ash, washing soda and for water softening generally. It should be pointed out that the production of these by-products is only ancillary to the carbonising of the coal for the production of either coke for the iron and steel industry or for gas for domestic and industrial purposes.

The carbonisation of coal is thus limited by the requirements of coke for the iron and steel industry and for other purposes and gas for domestic and industrial use. Coal is not carbonised especially for the production of by-products.

An electric generating station with a capacity of 300,000 kilowatts.

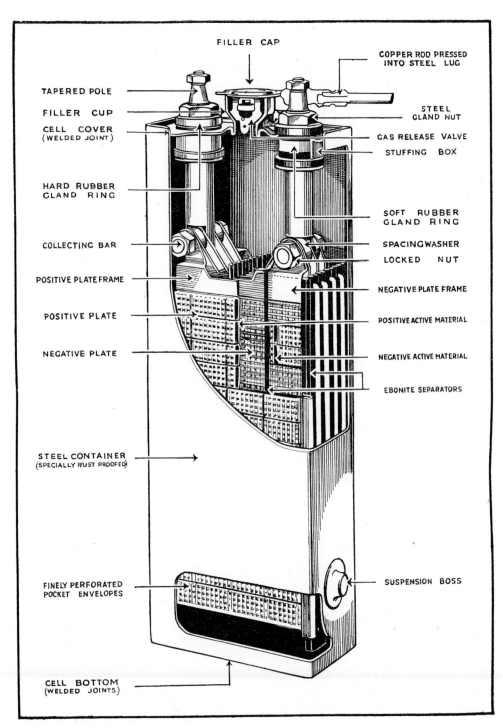

FILLER CAP

COPPER ROD PRESSED INTO STEEL LUG

TAPERED POLE

FILLER CUP

CELL COVER (WELDED JOINT)

STEEL GLAND NUT

GAS RELEASE VALVE

STUFFING BOX

HARD RUBBER GLAND RING

SOFT RUBBER GLAND RING

COLLECTING BAR

SPACINGWASHER

LOCKED NUT

POSITIVE PLATE FRAME

NEGATIVE PLATE FRAME

POSITIVE PLATE

POSITIVE ACTIVE MATERIAL

NEGATIVE PLATE

NEGATIVE ACTIVE MATERIAL

EBONITE SEPARATORS

STEEL CONTAINER (SPECIALLY RUST PROOFED)

FINELY PERFORATED POCKET ENVELOPES

SUSPENSION BOSS

CELL BOTTOM (WELDED JOINTS)

Sectional view of a nickel-cadmium train lighting cell.

WHAT AN ACCUMULATOR DOES

ELECTRICITY is all around us. We are largely, if not wholly, made of it ourselves, and so is all the matter that we know— the table on which I am writing, the paper on which this is printed, the dinner which we are going to eat to-night. Electricity, in fact, is everywhere. And the problem of electricity generation is not to *produce* electricity, but to "*extract*" it from the matter around us and to *harness* it to do useful work. From this it will be seen that electricity is not, in itself, a source of power, but rather a way of conveying power from one place to another. Elsewhere it is explained that coal is the first source of most of the electrical power used in this country, although in some other parts of the world the power represented by waterfalls is very largely employed instead. So we may say that coal gives engineers the power to extract electricity from matter, and that they convey the electricity to us along cables and wires. An accumulator is merely a way of storing up electricity so that we can carry its energy about. So it is that two of the chief uses of accumulators are to work portable wireless sets, and to work the lights, electric horns and self-starters of cars.

The simplest experiment in electricity is to rub a fountain-pen holder on one's sleeve and make the discovery that it will pick up small pieces of paper. Even this simple test teaches us two lessons, that electricity can often be extracted from matter by friction ; and that, having got it, we can make it do work for us—in this case pick up the pieces of paper.

It can be obtained as the result of chemical change or by means of the dynamo, where mechanical is turned into electrical energy in the cutting of lines of magnetic force. The oldest and simplest form of cell consists of a plate of copper with a plate of zinc standing in acid. Among the changes which take place is the dissolving of the zinc in the acid ; and among the results is the setting up of an electrical pressure between the copper and the zinc. This means that, if the two plates are connected, outside the cell, by a wire, electricity will flow from one plate to the other. Unfortunately it is not possible to give any simple explanation of why this should happen. It is, however, a fact ; and one that has been known for more than a hundred years.

All other cells work on a similar principle, including the batteries used to provide the current for electric torches, and the " high tension " batteries of battery-operated wireless sets. So also do the glass-encased cells which are used in many houses to provide the power for the domestic bell system. They have all, moreover, their limitations. Among the chief of their practical disadvantages is that the chemicals which are the source of their electrical energy, are soon used up. Cells are, in fact, merely a convenient means of " producing " electricity in small amounts and are not applicable to storage.

An accumulator is a cell which can be, as it were, re-wound. One series of chemical changes in the accumulator produces an electric current. The reverse series of chemical changes is brought about by driving an electric current through the accumulator in the opposite direction. This means that an accumulator which has been well treated can be brought back into its original condition by re-charging. It is rather an important distinction ; for, whereas the source of a cell's energy is chemical, the real source of an accumulator's energy are the mains from which it is charged. In fact, as has been explained, an accumulator is essentially a means of storage and not of production. In a car, for example, the first source of electrical energy is the engine. This drives a small dynamo which, during daylight running, is made to re-charge the accumulators, quite wrongly called batteries. Then, when electrical energy is wanted, either for lighting, to work the self-starter, or to sound the electric horn, the accumulators release part of their stored-up energy.

In its simplest possible form an accumulator might consist of two plates dipping into sulphuric acid, one plate being made of plain lead, and the other of lead coated with lead peroxide—lead combined with oxygen. As a current is taken from the accumulator, the acid attacks both plates, their surfaces being converted into lead sulphate. The electrical pressure is about 2.2 volts, compared with the 240 volts of most electric mains. When the pressure has fallen off to 1.8 volts, it is time for the accumulator to be re-charged. Then, as has already been said, the two plates are restored to their original condition ; that is to say, lead peroxide and lead.

In practice, an accumulator is built with a series of plates connected alternately in pairs. This is merely a way of increasing the area of the plates without making the accumulator too big, so that although an accumulator looks more complicated, it may still be thought of as having only two plates. To begin with, also, all the plates are made the same, being transformed into lead peroxide and lead only during the accumulator's first charging. All the plates are originally made as lead grids, in which the spaces are filled in with a special paste. The reason for this is that manufacturers want the plates to be spongy so that their effective area shall be as great as possible ; and it so happens that the arrangement

A storage battery consisting of 276 cells of large capacity.

described, followed by the normal process of charging, is one way of producing spongy plates.

Both these complications—the use of more than one pair of plates, and making the plates spongy—are merely ways of making the plates bigger. The bigger the plates, the more current can be taken from them. But there is one rather important point to notice. We can make the plates as big as we like ; but we shall not, by so doing, increase the electrical pressure beyond the 2.2 volts which even the smallest accumulator will give. If a bigger pressure is needed, more than one accumulator must be used ; and they must be joined together as it is said, "in series," so that greater pressures are built up. Most cars, for example, have six accumulators, giving a total of 12 volts, but for some cars 6 volts are considered satisfactory. You may have noticed that the terminals of most accumulators are marked either in red and blue, or " plus " and " minus." These are conventional signs used to show at a glance in which direction the current will flow.

Lead plates immersed in sulphuric acid do not represent the only way in which an accumulator can be made, and other metals with other solutions may be employed. In one important variety a solution of

By courtesy of]   [Joseph Lucas Ltd.

Battery section showing inter-cell partitions, acid level indicators and combined vent plug and drip cup.

potassium hydrate is used instead of sulphuric acid, and plates consisting of perforated steel envelopes are used for both positive (+) and negative (−). The pockets of the positive plate contain a mixture of nickel hydroxide with other substances to improve conductivity, while the steel envelopes of the negative plate contain a mixture of cadmium and iron oxides. The electrical pressure obtained from accumulators of this type is approximately 1.2 volts per accumulator and, therefore, a number of accumulators have to be used in series in the ordinary manner.

As steel is so much stronger than lead, the nickel cadmium alkaline accumulator is useful for undertaking very strenuous duties such as in providing stand-by current for trolley buses. The accumulators are sufficient to propel these heavy buses, weighing thirteen and a half tons, when they are turned round at the termini, or for emergency propulsion in the event of failure of the main supply.

The subject of electrical storage is one which still attracts many experimenters, and there is little doubt that the future will see development in the direction of capacity maintenance over long periods by means of apparatus which is relatively light or compact in relation to present standards.

The programme engineer in a listening room during rehearsal.

HOW A GREAT BROADCAST IS ARRANGED

THOUGH it takes you only one hour to listen to the Christmas Day round-the-world broadcast, this wonderful programme gathered from the four corners of the earth requires nearly six months to prepare. It is a hot day in June when officials at Broadcasting House first discuss the form the programme will take and appoint its producer.

When the theme has been decided and the general shape and content been agreed, letters are sent to the other broadcasting organisations which are to take part giving them a general outline of the programme. The form each individual contribution should take is suggested on general lines only and the actual subject and treatment is left to the local producer. Naturally the subject he chooses is associated with his country. The sound of the Niagara Falls was sent from Canada during the first of these broadcasts in 1932 and, among other interesting things, we have heard messages from refugees in Germany and the bells of the Church of the Holy Sepulchre from Jerusalem. The items must be kept very short because only a few minutes can be allotted to each of them.

After the individual overseas producers have decided the form that their contribution is to take they send their scripts to the producer in London. He arranges these overseas items in the desired order interspersed with items from the British Isles. This programme is always transmitted to many of the countries taking part and they take great interest in

The 500-ft. mast-radiator of the B.B.C.'s London transmitting station.

hearing the greetings from Britain. The various items take the form of messages from shepherds in the mountains, lighthouse keepers and miners in the pits.

The musical background must also be written and arranged, and the dialogue knitting the programme together has to be prepared, sometimes this is in the form of poetry and a famous actor is employed to say it.

Many hours are spent calculating the timing and the fitting together of the various items, for this important programme must be arranged and synchronised to the split second. The task is all the more complicated because when it is the afternoon of Christmas

HOW A BROADCAST IS ARRANGED

Day in London it is early morning in Canada and tea-time in South Africa. In India people are having their evening meal while in Australia it is after midnight. As a large part of the overseas programme is received over Post Office commercial radio telephone circuits, the time of the programme has to be chosen so that these are available. These short wave radio circuits which are used for normal overseas telephone calls are affected by all kinds of climatic conditions and by the state of the Ionosphere. The Ionosphere is the region which surrounds the earth beyond the stratosphere and, from it, transmitted radio waves are reflected. Thus when one circuit—say to Australia—is at its best the others may be totally unsuitable for reception. The engineers originally suggested that

[B.B.C. Copyright.

PRODUCING THE NOISE OF A TRAIN

The girl moves wire brushes over a drumskin for the puffing of the engine ; the man in the middle rubs a hollow box on sandpaper for the sound of steam escaping ; and the man on the right moves a roller skate over a stick for the sound of the wheels.

171

between two and three o'clock in the afternoon would be the best time and the many successful broadcasts have proved them right.

At last the producer makes his final plans and proceeds to conduct rehearsals. While the rehearsals of the individual items are in progress the producer is in a soundproof room listening to the programme over a loudspeaker. There are a number of

[B.B.C. Copyright.

A programme rehearsal.

microphones in the studio for the various actors taking part and he can switch from one to the other as he desires. He is also connected to the studio by means of a microphone so that he can talk with the performers in the studio about any little point which needs alteration. The performers can reply to him over the ordinary microphones. During rehearsal he marks the script so that during the actual broadcast the programme engineer can balance the microphones and the studio sound output as the producer has planned it. The programme engineer controls the output of sound from the studio because the transmitter cannot handle too great a volume and a great crescendo from the orchestra

Miners speaking on a B.B.C. " Round the World " programme on Christmas Day.

would overload it and cause distortion. Similar rehearsals are being carried out at all the overseas stations. When it comes to rehearsing the overseas programmes with the B.B.C. producer in London, he is connected to the country concerned through the Post Office radio telephone transmitters at Rugby or Baldock. He listens closely to the transmission and makes notes of any alterations

[B.B.C. Copyright.

The transmitter control desk and part of the transmitting equipment.

he thinks are necessary. He is able to speak to the studio of the overseas broadcasting station and so can advise and discuss with them the alterations he requires.

At the final rehearsal special disc recordings are made. These are similar to gramophone records and are necessary as a standby in case the radio link cannot be completed on Christmas Day. If, for instance, the interference on the overseas circuit to New Zealand is so great that reception is impossible then, on a given signal, the engineers can switch in the record taken at the final rehearsal so that the programme can proceed in the arranged order.

(*Above*) This equipment records programmes in case of a breakdown.
(*Below*) Producer and programme engineer at the control panel.

HOW A BROADCAST IS ARRANGED

In the past, recordings have never been used where it has been possible to give direct transmission. Of course this is sometimes impossible through lack of transmitting facilities at certain out-of-the-way places. In these cases pre-recordings have to be made and brought to Britain in time for the broadcast.

At the various regional studios rehearsals of their contributions are taking place, and special lines are being provided so that the outside broadcasts such as the voice of a shepherd on his lonely fell or the bells of a famous cathedral, can be heard. In many cases ordinary telephone lines are used, though these are specially tested by the Post Office as well as the B.B.C. engineers. Great care has to be taken to see that these circuits do not disturb the programme in any way and are free from noise. Permanent lines exist between the Queen's study and the B.B.C. in order that she may take part in this broadcast and send Christmas greetings to the Commonwealth. These lines, too, are given a final test.

In producing a programme of this kind, where the various contributions originate in such widely separated places, there has to be a common control point to which all the items can be brought, and from which they can be sent out again as a whole to be transmitted to the ether.

One of the dramatic control rooms at Broadcasting House is used for this, and in it the producer sits with the control of all the incoming programmes at his finger-tips on a large panel. All the lines carrying the different items are brought into the Transmission Control Room. The several circuits from the various studios in Broadcasting House itself, where people are waiting to make their contributions at the appointed moment, the announcer in one, the narrator in another, the orchestra in a third and so on, are connected to the Dramatic Control Panel. Special circuits are provided from the Recording Room ready to substitute for any of the items should an emergency arise. The lines from the various parts of the British Isles and the lines from the radio transmitters at Rugby or Baldock all terminate on the knobs which cover the panel before the producer.

Some of the circuits are amplified and balanced before going to the Dramatic Control Panel and from here return to the Transmission Control Room to be amplified and sent to the various transmitting stations radiating the programme on the various wave-

A TELEVISION STUDIO

THE BOULDER DAM IN ARIZONA

[B.B.C. Copyright.

The sound of horses' hooves and jangling harness is produced by hollow wooden blocks and bunches of keys.

lengths. The switching operations of the radio telephone circuits are often complicated because in addition to bringing in one circuit promptly after another, arrangements have to be made for the whole of the programme to be transmitted to some of the countries concerned.

As a rule people in the broadcasting studios are notified when it is time to begin giving their items by the glowing of a red lamp which is controlled from the Transmission Control Room. In the case of the Christmas broadcast, those taking part in the studios are able to hear, by means of loudspeakers, what is taking place when they themselves are not actually performing. As the time for their turn arrives a green light operated from the Dramatic Control Panel is flicked in their studio, their loudspeaker is faded out, and the microphone is switched in.

At last everything is as complete as it can be. The recordings taken are ready for use, the lines tested and the various control circuits set up. The producer takes his seat at the panel in the Dramatic Control Room with his script beside him and—most important—his stop-watch before his eyes, so that he can ensure that each item is faded in and out in exact time and order. Detailed instructions have also been issued to the controlling engineers at the various switching points, the radio telephone stations, the regional studios, the recording rooms and the studios. One mistake in the timing would probably ruin the whole programme, for if one item is allowed to over-run its allotted time then it would have to be cut off to make way for the next one.

The producer brings in the various items as required and builds up the programme, controlling and combining the word pictures, the effects, and the music, etc., into one artistic whole. The arranged programme goes via one circuit from the Dramatic Control Panel to the Transmission Control Room where it is amplified and sent out to the transmitters.

The whole programme is a wonderful demonstration of the advance of modern communication engineering. It illustrates the strong links which radio-telephony has forged between the Mother Country and the Commonwealth and shows the paramount position of London as the centre of the world's communication network.

[B.B.C. Copyright.

Reading the nine o'clock news.

Breaking up the road surface with drills.

[*Mirrorpic.*]

HOW ROADS ARE MADE

THE " Road Problem " is a common topic of discussion to-day, and most people have their own ideas as to how roads could be made safer, or better able to deal with the ever-increasing number of motor vehicles. But roads must not only be safe and wide. They must also be strong. The strains put upon a busy thoroughfare by the continual flow of traffic are tremendous. The Romans, great road builders though they were, had not to contend with anything comparable with modern traffic. Road construction and repair, since the invention of the motor car in its various forms, has become a major industry.

The condition of the roads of England a hundred and fifty years ago seems incredible to modern motorists who have almost forgotten what dust is like. At the beginning of the 19th century, roads were so bad that, in many cases, it was impossible to tell where the road ended and the fields began. Journeys that are now accomplished in hours, took days. In summer the dust made travelling intolerable and in winter the mud made it almost impossible except on the busiest highways. And those were the days when there was not even the alternative of travelling by railway or air. No wonder most people stayed at home.

179

HOW ROADS ARE MADE

Part of the trouble was that we were not prepared to spend money on roads, but most of it was merely that we did not know how to make roads. A great deal of money was spent, but the new roads were useless almost as soon as they were constructed.

Except for such pioneers in scientific road-making as John McAdam and Telford, the motor car could never have reached its present stage of development. A century and a half ago a journey was an almost intolerable agony because of the bumping, and accidents owing to broken axles were frequent. We think of road accidents as a modern thing, but owing to the condition of the roads they were quite common in the days of stage coaches.

John McAdam, who died just a century ago, realised that the then existing principles of road making were wrong. All his life he studied roads scientifically and his fame is commemorated in that word " macadam," even though it is spelt differently. McAdam came to the conclusion that great strength could be obtained from small pieces of stone packed tightly, an idea which in those days was revolutionary. To-day, compressed rock enters into the construction of many highways. McAdam also realised that no road would last if it was not properly drained. Hence he advocated that the road should always be rather higher than the surrounding land and that it should have drains at the side. We now take the greatest care of our roads and although they are not permitted to be cambered so steeply as in pre-motor car days, it is comparatively rare to see any water lying about for long periods.

The surface of roads is very important to-day, not only because we demand smooth riding in our cars, but also because it is realised that once the surface has been broken, the whole road begins to go to pieces. Once a small hole is made, each succeeding vehicle going over it knocks out another little stone or chip. In a few hours, on a busy road, a little hole has become a pit that jerks every passing car. Until the coming of motor cars, most roads were surfaced with broken stone, much in the way suggested by John McAdam, who said that all pieces of stone should be of very nearly the same size and no piece should weigh more than six ounces.

The stone breaker whom we used to see at work in his protecting glasses at the roadside, has now disappeared. All kinds of surfaces are being tried. Some roads are of cement and concrete, others are surfaced with pitch and small stones, macadamised. Others again, chiefly in large towns, are surfaced with blocks of tarred wood. Rubber and iron are other surfaces that are being tested. Probably the perfect road surface for all purposes has yet to be discovered. New problems have arisen. For example, a modern surface should

By courtesy of]   [*The Caterpillar Tractor Co. Ltd.*

Using a bulldozer to widen the road.

not glare back the
headlights of cars at
night or dazzle when
it is wet. Again, skid-
ding is one of the
commonest causes of
road accidents and the
road is often to blame.
Scattering gravel when
it is wet seems to be a
crude method of re-
ducing slipperiness.

To watch a gang
of workmen mending
a road or making a
new surface, the pro-
cess may not appear
very scientific. The
men seem to mix con-
crete or lay the stone
rather by rule of
thumb methods. But
in actual fact, modern

By courtesy of]   *[The Caterpillar Tractor Co. Ltd.*
A team of tractors making a new road.

road building is highly technical. Much of the work is done before
the actual construction begins. One of the secrets of strong roads
is good materials of known quality. All materials employed for road
making to-day are, therefore, laboratory tested before being used. In
many cases the experiments are carried out by specially-devised
apparatus and are very interesting.

By making up a specimen taken at random and allowing it to
set, the cement used in road making is also tested for tensile strength.
The "brick" is then placed in a machine which tears it apart,
measuring the pull required to reach breaking point. The degree of
strength required may vary between six hundred and nine hundred
pounds to the square inch, and higher figures have been attained.

Small stones, varying in size from mere pieces of grit to pieces
three inches round, are submitted to tests. A sample is taken and
tried for size by being passed through sieves. Single stones are
examined microscopically. The blending of sand or stone with

cement is also carried out scientifically, the exact proportions required for the work in hand being calculated. It may seem that the workmen are careless, but the containers for sand and cement are of known size and ensure that each batch is mixed in the right proportions.

In concrete road building use is made of a steel mesh which looks almost like wire-netting laid flat. This serves the same strengthening purposes as the rods and bars of iron in ferro-concrete, but actually these steel meshes are exceedingly strong. They are not nets, but are cut out of blank pieces of steel without any welds or joins, the whole being one continuous piece of metal of immense strength. An advantage is that a small piece of road can be taken up to lay, for example, a gas pipe, without destroying the bond of the remaining part of expanded steel mesh.

Even the tar laid on the roads is analysed to ensure that it is of the right consistency and quality. Tar that is too volatile will melt in hot weather and make the roads " sticky." The tar is tested by being broken up into its various constituents and by being pulled apart in the same way as cement, at different temperatures. Bitumen is also very carefully examined.

Complete sections of road can be tested to find out if the materials used and the method of construction will give a long life. One way to test a road is to lay it and see what happens after five

[*Fox Photos.*

This machine cuts cylindrical cores from concrete roads to test strength and durability.

or ten years. But we cannot always wait so long to see the result of an experiment. There has been devised, therefore, a testing machine in which a heavy wheel is kept revolving continuously over a small circle of specimen road, or a piece of surface may be revolved under the wheel. The real problem to-day is not to produce a surface that will wear well, as we have several of this type, but one that will be skid-proof in any kind of weather. Curiously enough, it has been found that some roads are more slippery when wet in summer than in winter.

The roads of the near future will be wider and safer. Pedestrians and cyclists may each have their special tracks, and motorists going in opposite directions will be separated by a hedge or guard running down the middle of the road. A hedge would also serve the purpose of preventing dazzle from headlights. Higher speed with greater safety will be possible on these roads, for it is probable that they will be floodlit or even, one day, may carry some method of transmitting power to every vehicle.

By courtesy of]   *[The Caterpillar Tractor Co. Ltd.*

Constructing a road in a remote part of Mexico.

[*Photopress.*

The " made-up " pages in the chases on the " stone."

HOW A BOOK IS MADE

A PART from those actually engaged in the making of books, few people realise, when they pick up a volume and open it, what a number of processes there are in turning out such a thing, from the point at which the printer receives the manuscript until, bound and wrappered, the completed book is ready for sale.

First of all, the printer " makes a cast-off," which means that he finds the number of words in the author's typescript and then decides what style of type is required and how many lines must go to a page in order to make a book of a certain number of pages. The printer reckons by sheets of sixty-four pages, thirty-two pages on each side, and endeavours to make the book an even number of " sixty-fours " or " thirty-twos " ; that is, 256, 288, or 320 pages.

The first few pages are known as the " prelims," or preliminary matter to the actual story ; they consist of title pages, list of contents, and possibly a preface or introduction. They are usually numbered in roman numerals, the story continuing on in arabic figures.

Having settled the size and style of type to be used, the printer composes and prints a specimen page, showing exactly how it will appear in the bound book, and sends it to the publisher for his approval. The typesetting of the book is then commenced on a typesetting machine. Before these machines were invented, all books were set by hand. The machines set and make type seven times faster than the hand compositor can set it. The machines themselves place the type on galleys (long strips of metal with three raised sides), which hold about one hundred and forty lines. A proof of this type is then taken on a hand press, and the printer's reader goes carefully over it to find any mistakes in setting. A compositor then makes these corrections. The printer then divides the type on the galley into pages, with so many lines to a page, adds a headline to each, and ties a cord round the page, holding it together. Sometimes, to make a greater number of pages, or to make the type easier to read, thin strips of metal known as " leads " are placed between each line.

When sixty-four pages have been " made-up," they are placed on the " stone," which is a bench with a very smooth iron surface, and a frame of steel, known as a " chase," is placed around each

A minder scanning an early sheet from a flatbed printing machine in the machine room.

By courtesy of]   *[Butler & Tanner Ltd.*

Sheets coming off a rotary printing machine. The girl on the right is collecting and stacking the printed and folded sheets.

sixteen pages. The correct space is placed between each page, and then, with wedge-shaped " quoins," the forme is locked-up so that the whole sixteen pages may be carried to the hand press for proofs to be taken and sent to the author or publisher.

The proofs being finally passed, the formes are placed on the presses for printing. Sixty-four pages, or sometimes as many as one hundred and twenty-eight pages, are usually printed together, and are so laid on the machine that, when the sheet of paper is printed on both sides, it folds to make sections each usually consisting of sixteen pages.

The correct placing of the formes in the great machine is a very delicate business, for, while the machine is running, pressure of the type against the paper must be perfectly even. When this " make-ready," as it is called, is satisfactory, yet another proof is taken by giving the machine a preliminary run, and then, if all is in order, the machine is set to work in earnest, and runs off the number of copies required.

HOW A BOOK IS MADE

This is the initial printing from the *original* type. If it is antici-pated that further editions of the book will be needed, what is known as a matrix of the type is taken, usually, to save the expense of keeping the metal of which the type is composed lying idle between printings, though sometimes the type itself is kept " standing," as it is called. The matrix consists of sheets of absorbent and tissue paper pasted together, laid wet on the type, beaten in with a brush and then baked hard. A metal casting can be taken from it when required, and used instead of type in the printing machine.

Yet another method of reproduction for further editions of a book consists in photographing the pages, and making metal plates from the photographs. These plates are then mounted and set together in the same way as the original type or matrix castings and printed. This process is known as photo-lithography.

But now, when all this is done, the result is merely a series of flat sheets of paper, printed on both sides, and that is a long way from the bound and finished book. Sometimes, but rarely, the printer folds the sheets. Usually, they go as they are from the printing works to the binders, and here undergo a fresh set of operations which involve the use of just as clever and intricate machinery, and skilled work, as went to the making of the printed sheets.

Now, examine the back of almost any book you choose. Bend the whole book open wide, and look carefully at the way in which the pages are set against each other, and you will find that the book is made up of separate sections, each containing, as a rule, sixteen pages. When the big sixty-four page sheets come to the binder, they are fed first of all into a folding machine, an ingenious piece of mechanism which folds each sheet in half, folds it again and yet again until there are four of these sections of sixteen pages apiece. End papers (the pages just inside the front and rear covers of the bound book) are now pasted on to the first and last sections, and any plates or illustrations are pasted or folded in. The sections are numbered or lettered in sequence so that they can be easily " collated," that is, gathered together in the proper order, checked to see that they are correct and made up as complete books in loose sections.

The books then go to the sewing machine to be sewn together with thread ; some of the larger and heavier books having tapes added to make them more secure. And the way in which this

(*Above*) An automatic casemaking machine at work.
(*Below*) Folding machines in a book-binding works.

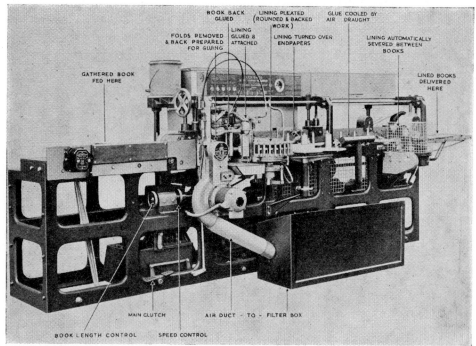

By courtesy of]   [The Book Machinery Co. Ltd.

AN UNSEWN BINDER.

With this machine, books can be bound without first being sewn.

sewing machine takes in and stitches them perfectly and turns them out, is little short of marvellous. Still, on emerging, they are far too thick in appearance : the book at this stage is a very fat, puffy-looking thing.

It is passed on, now, for one of the simplest and yet most important operations of all, known as " nipping," or " pressing." As the press opens, the operator in charge thrusts in the books from, say, two to four at a time, and the jaws close together and flatten the copies, squeezing out the air which keeps the pages apart, and pressing them down with its enormous force. The machine works as regularly as the pendulum of a grandfather clock, and the books are taken out and stacked ready for passing on to the next set of operations. The binder counts the initial " nipping " one of the most important processes of his work. By this time, the book is beginning to take shape, but, of course, without its covers.

After " pressing " or " nipping," the book goes to the cutter and the three sides are trimmed square. Then the back is glued and lined with " mull," a kind of thick muslin, the book then passing on to the " rounding-and-backing " machine, where the back or " spine " is rounded. After this the back of the book is glued once more, and a second lining, this time of strong paper, is put on, to give additional strength. It is now ready for the covers or cases.

So far, we have seen nothing of these covers, or cases as the binder calls them. They come to the works—for an ordinary cloth-bound book—in great sheets of millboard, which are cut up to the size required. There are two pieces of millboard to each bound book, and one piece of cloth a little more than double the size of each piece of millboard, the three are fed together into a machine, between guides which make certain that they are in their proper places. The cloth passes over a roller which applies exactly the right amount of glue, and then, click, and hey presto ! out comes the cover with the cloth neatly folded over and glued to the sections of millboard.

But it is just a plain cover which might be used for any book.

Feeding the stitched sheets into a rounding-and-backing machine.

It passes on to a press which stamps whatever lettering is required on the front cover and " spine " or back of the book. In most cases, this is a single process printing black type, but sometimes gold or more than one colour is used. In this latter case, the colours are printed on the cover separately, ink of a different colour being used for each printing.

Now, with the covers dried and ready, comes the final assembling. The books are fed into a machine called a casing-in machine. A pile of cases are placed at one end : these are automatically fed in one at a time, and the machine places them over the book, which in the meantime has received a coating of glue on its two outer sheets, which adhere to the covering case and give that neat finish which we know, hiding away the canvas and tapes that hold the book together. Then, stacked in presses, the finished books go off for their final pressing : the contents of each press is subjected to a tremendous pressure, and the press is clamped at that pressure and the books are left in it until required. Each book is examined

By courtesy of]　　　　　　　　　　　　　　　[Butler & Tanner Ltd.

An automatic blocking machine at work.

A case-making machine in operation.

carefully as it is taken out, to see that it is correct in all respects.

When that time comes, the books have to be given their paper " jackets " which keep the cloth covers clean and add to the attractive appearance of volumes on stalls and in shop windows. The printing of these, usually in three or more colours, is usually a complicated business in itself, involving the making of a " plate " or " block " for each colour, and as many printings as there are colours used. In three-colour printing, the primary colours, red, blue and yellow are used, one to each " block," and between them they make up the various shades seen on the finished jacket. Sometimes only two " blocks " are required, the finished jacket having no red in it, or no blue, or no yellow, as the case may be. For very high quality work, as many as seven or even more colours may be used, involving as many separate printings, but this is rare with book-jackets.

Last of all, the books themselves are taken out from their final pressing and the jackets are put on. And, if you want to know whether this is a skilled operation, try cutting a sheet of paper to the size of a book-jacket, and see how long it takes to get it folded over the cover with the correct amount of overlap back and front. It will probably take about ten times as long as a skilled operator would require—and then the chances are that it is not on exactly as it should be ! And yet this is about the simplest of all the processes that go to the making of the book you buy and read.

Setting the type.

In this spacious and well-equipped kitchen, meals for four thousand people are prepared daily.

HOW A BIG HOTEL CATERS AND COOKS

A S you sit enjoying your supper in the restaurant of a big hotel, you little think that the lunch you will eat at one o'clock next day is already being planned. In an office upstairs several men are gathered round a desk planning the dishes with which you will be served, and setting in motion the complicated but perfectly organized machinery that will ensure the punctual arrival of your meal at the table in sixteen hours' time. Rationing, purchase tax and shortage of equipment, the Catering Wages Order and staffing problems were post-war factors which have revolutionised the hotelier's business. Nevertheless, intricate planning and attention to many details are still the foundations for the individual style and high reputation of the big hotel.

The chef is the supreme head of all the culinary arrangements. First of all, in consultation with the head-waiters, he decides on the menu, remembering what foods are in season, what variation of dishes will make the widest choice for you, within the hotel's price range. Then he writes the menu out and sends it to be printed on the cards on your table. He consults the assistant manager as to approximately how many people may be expected to want lunches next day.

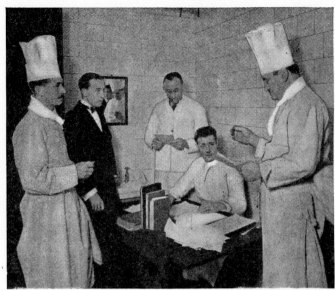

By courtesy of]   *[The Strand Hotel Ltd.*

The head chef plans the next day's menus with the store-keeper, the under-chef and head waiter.

The visitors' register in the reception-office tells the manager how many guests are actually staying in the hotel, but to this number he must add an estimate of probable " outside " guests, which naturally depends on the weather and the time of the year, and whether there is any particular attraction such as an exhibition in the vicinity that day. Consulting the record-book for the corresponding day of the previous week and the corresponding week last year also helps the manager to make his careful calculations, and he is usually able to tell the chef to within about a score how many meals will need to be provided.

Then the chef goes down to the domestic quarters to interview the head store-keeper, who acts as buyer for all the foodstuffs. In some hotels, he sends down his requirements to the goods office, which orders the foodstuffs, receives them when they are delivered, and conveys them to the stores. The stores department is an enormous place, comprising dozens of different rooms in which the various commodities are kept. Some rooms, including the dairy, are interwalled with stone and fitted with marble shelves to keep the contents in perfect freshness. The dry grocery room holds tiers of stainless steel drawers and bins full of cocoa and sugar and such. Every room is specially air-conditioned and has heating or refrigerating pipes so that the correct temperature can be evenly maintained, no matter what the weather is like.

In every store-room the contents are arranged in strict alphabetical order. Thus in the fruit-room you find the boxes of apples immediately inside, while the racks of pineapples are much farther along. This facilitates clerking, for the exact quantity of each different kind of stores has to be stated under its letter on the big framed index-sheet which hangs behind the door.

The chef and his kitchen clerk reckon out just what ingredients will be needed for the requisite number of lunches—how much meat, how many pears, how much flour and spice for the sauce, how much cooking fat and so on. They write out all these amounts on official requisition forms, which the head store-keeper or goods clerk takes, so that he knows exactly what must be delivered to the kitchens next morning.

The assistant store-keepers are then called to the head's office, bringing with them the day's index-sheets from the various rooms of which they have charge. Thus the head is able to see what is in stock and can estimate how much he requires to buy to make up the quantities necessary to balance the chef's requisitions. Some hotels have their own farms which supply much of the produce they use, and all have

By courtesy of]   [The Strand Hotel Ltd.

Laying the tables.

at least one outside buyer. Some large hotels have as many as three. He takes the order-forms from the head store-keeper and visits the wholesale meat market and the green-grocery market and similar centres when they commence business in the early hours of the morning, inspecting the produce with an expert eye before he buys. Everything is delivered to the hotel between eight and ten and is passed along to the various store-rooms.

Then each assistant store-keeper takes out the quantity of his commodities ordered by the head and sends it to the kitchens. Here the chef, with his clerk in attendance to book up its arrival, is waiting to receive the produce and distribute it among his numerous under-cooks. There is the soup cook, the fish cook, the vegetable cook, the pastry cook and many others, each concerned with the preparation of certain things only and working in his separate department, an individual kitchen contained in the gigantic general kitchen. Then there is the still-room, where cheese, toast, coffee, pats of butter and other light items on the menu are made ready. There is the grill which may well work by infra-red rays to cook grills very rapidly, and the big pantry where oysters are opened and salads chopped and dressed and fruit arranged in decorative baskets ready for the table.

Soon everybody is working busily in the kitchen, which usually has a high domed ceiling and special ventilation to carry away the cooking odours and special non-slipping rubber floor-covering, which is also fireproof, since so many different stoves and ovens and roasting spits, etc., are in operation. There are numerous machines which help the cooks in their tasks. There is the automatic meat-chopper and the moving tray on which long loaves of bread travel to be sliced by a descending guillotine knife. There is the tubular machine into which potatoes are placed to travel round a central blade and emerge neatly peeled, and the whirring pudding-mixer with its metal spokes like a miniature octopus. In the scullery adjoining the vegetable cook's department are wire cages in which such things as cabbages and lettuces are placed to be thoroughly washed by rotation in deep tanks of salted water. The chef has given each of his under-cooks a requisition form telling them just how many pies or portions of spinach or pairs of grilled cutlets and so forth they are responsible for sending to the service-room.

While the cooks are occupied, the restaurant itself is being prepared for lunch-time. The head-waiter has allotted each of his men to a certain "station" or number of adjacent tables referred to by a distinguishing letter, and the waiter now takes a card bearing the corresponding letter to the pantry-stores, where he receives the cutlery, linen, cruets, occasional china and glasses and so on for his particular station. In some hotels, of course, the waiters have "permanent stations".

As the waiters are laying the tables, the cooks are adding the final touches to their dishes. A little before lunchtime, the chef,

By courtesy of]   *[The Strand Hotel Ltd.*
Waiters pass along the service counter collecting crockery, cutlery, food and drink. They enter at one end by a door swinging inward, and leave at the other end by a door swinging outward.

who has been generally supervising the kitchen work, takes up his stand in the big service-room, which is fitted with long tables with massive galvanized metal frames and strong wooden tops. Opposite the tables are rows of hot-plates, broad copper sheets usually heated by electric current passing beneath. As the cook finishes his particular contribution to the menu, he places the huge containers on a trolley which a kitchen boy wheels along to the service-room ready to be dished up into individual portions. Perhaps the container stands on the hot-plate to keep nicely warm until served. If it is a cold dish, then one of the servers, who are each responsible for a single item of the meal as are the cooks, will get busy at a side-table dividing it out on to the china plates ready for the waiters to serve. One table belongs to the carver, who, with a speed and dexterity that is truly amazing, wields his great knives and forks upon the various sizzling joints as they are lifted down from the hot-plate.

To facilitate the speed of the service and ensure that nobody gets in anybody else's way, " one-way traffic " prevails in this important room. The waiter enters from the restaurant by one door and drops his tray on to a metal rack, sliding it along past the servers, who supply him with their particular dish in exchange for a requisition note—these are the little slips of paper on which you see him scribbling as he takes your order at the table. When he gets to the end of the rack, which runs all round the room, he lifts up his laden tray and carries it off into the restaurant through a second door, which only opens outwards. As he later comes to write out your bill, he must remember to charge as many items as he has given requisition notes, otherwise the final kitchen and office cash accounts will not balance.

By courtesy of]   *[J. Lyons & Co. Ltd.*

One of the restaurants in a modern hotel.

By courtesy of]   [*A. G. Spalding & Bros. Ltd.*

Shaping the blade with a spokeshave.

MAKING CRICKET BATS AND TENNIS RACKETS

"WIELDING the willow" is a very old expression for using a cricket bat, and to this day English willow is the only wood used for the blade of a bat. The firm, even texture of the wood, its lightness, and the fact that it is one of the least likely to split after proper seasoning, render it more suitable than any other for the cricketer's use. A tree is selected, felled at the right size, and sawn into lengths and then split into clefts or billets, which are placed in stacks for seasoning, and when the wood is well seasoned, it is taken for use by the bat-maker, and, at first, very roughly shaped for its purpose.

Then there is the handle to be considered. This is composed of strips of cane, squared to fit closely to each other, and bound and glued together : in a good bat there may be nine, or a dozen, or even more of these strips, forming a square stick of cane, considerably thicker than the finished handle. In the final shaping, nearly half the cane becomes waste in the form of chips, and only the core of the original composite stick remains to give the necessary resilience to the bat, and to help to reduce the shock of its impact against a ball.

Now, for the fitting together of the two, a deep, narrow V-shaped cut is made in the top of the blade, of which the shoulders are carried up, also

By courtesy of]   [A. G. Spalding & Bros. Ltd.

Fitting the handle to the blade.

in a sort of V-section, to assist in gripping the handle. This latter is shaped to fit in the cut that has been made in the blade, and the two are fitted together. Here comes the delicate part of bat-making, for the wedge of cane must be an absolutely perfect fit in the blade : there is no pinning together, no fastening of any kind except for the thinnest possible coating of fine quality glue : after fitting these two parts together, a clamp is tightened on the top end of the blade, and kept in position until the joint has thoroughly set. Then the bat is placed in a lathe and the rough, square-section cane handle turned and cut to length.

After this comes the final shaping. The blade of the bat is shaped nicely by plane, drawknife and spokeshave, sandpapered, and then given its polish by rubbing down with a length of cane or bone, or similar hard—but not too hard—polishing medium. In its final dimensions, a cricket bat for test or county play must not exceed thirty-eight inches in length, and the span of the blade at its widest part must not be more than four-and-a-quarter inches.

After this comes the cording of the cane handle, and a very brief inspection of the handle of a first-class bat will reveal this as a highly-skilled operation. It is, too, a very necessary one, for each time that a ball is struck with any force there is a certain amount of " give " among the segments of cane composing the handle of the bat, and if the waxed thread binding were not done evenly and at the right tension, they would soon separate from each other and render the bat useless. By standing a bat on end and looking down at the top of the handle, it is easy to see how many strips of cane have been used in making it ; the top of a first-class bat shows as a chessboard pattern of tiny squares ; a cheap bat may show four dividing lines or less—or even no lines at all if one thick cane has been used to form the handle. The fine cane used in the making of high-quality bats is imported from the East Indies, and is a costly product.

To preserve a cricket bat in good condition, the user is told to oil the blade, but never to apply oil at the joint of blade and handle. Also, never stand a bat upright after oiling, or in oil, otherwise the oil will trickle down to the toe and make the toe soft and heavy and will spoil the

By courtesy of] *[A. G. Spalding & Bros. Ltd.*
Binding a hockey stick handle with coloured twines.

balance. This is a very necessary caution, for moisture of any kind, oil included, is fatal to glue, and if either oil or water gets at the joint for any length of time, the joint will be spoilt. And in that simple joint is the very essence of the bat-maker's skill: with no more than the thinnest layer of glue, the cane is fitted into the willow, one smooth, flat surface adhering to the other so perfectly that the two remain one even if the player sends the ball clean out of the ground with every hit he makes. If only out of respect for the maker's skill, that joint is worth preserving.

Thus, when oiling the blade of a cricket bat, do not apply oil too near the joint of blade and handle.

Now, just as willow is essential for the making of cricket bats, so is ash, and in a lesser degree beech, necessary for tennis rackets. Especially in the case of ash, there is a toughness of grain which permits of bending to the oval shape with which we are all familiar, the frame of the racket through which the gut is strung. This frame may consist of anything from one strip of wood up to seven

Cutting a plank to make the racket frame.

or even more very thin strips, and, where more than one compose the frame, they are at first flat strips, glued together under pressure in the same way that ordinary plywood is made, except that in the layers designed to go out to the world as tennis racket frames, the grain of the

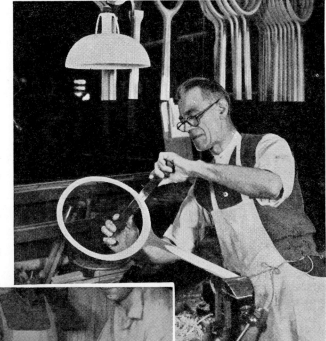

Trimming the shaped frame.

wood is all running the same way, and far greater care is used in selecting, testing, and fitting the various layers to each other than is the case in making plywood.

The length of each prepared plank is a little more than the overall measurement of a finished

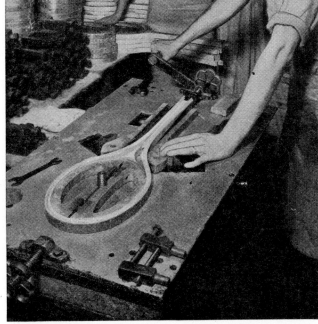

Photos by courtesy of]   [A. G. Spalding & Bros. Ltd.

Shaping the frame.

205

racket: that is, if you ran a measuring tape up one side of the handle of a racket, round the strung frame and down the other side of the handle, and then added, say, four inches to the total, you would get the length of the prepared strip. It is bent to shape without the aid of steam (as in the old method where a single piece of ash was alone used), the triangular piece of wood to which the frame is eventually screwed on either side is fitted in position, and the bent strips are securely clamped and put aside to set, so that the frame will keep its shape in the processes it has to undergo.

Then, set and ready, the shaped frame, now roughly square in section, is still a far different thing from the finely-finished product. Each frame is spokeshaved, scraped, and sandpapered down to the almost oval section which we see when the strings are in position, and four strips of wood, beech as a rule, though other woods are used as well, are fitted over the parallel strips of framing which make the foundation of the handle. And in all this shaping, particular attention has to be paid to weight and balance: there is no rigid standard of weight as in some requisites of sport, for a tennis player chooses a racket of a weight to suit himself or herself, within a limit of ounces, but balance is a very important particular in manufacture. It is corrected, in some cases, by the insertion of a tiny slug of lead at the end of the handle, but the presence or absence of this depends on the racket itself, and the relative weights of the different parts.

Cane is not a necessity in racket making, for the elasticity demanded of a cricket bat is not necessary for striking the lighter and more resilient tennis ball, while, in addition, there is a certain amount of " give " in the stringing of a racket, and in the tennis ball itself.

Stringing is a delicate and highly-skilled operation: the vertical strings are first threaded on to the frame and tightened, and then the cross-strings, set alternately in front of and behind each vertical string, help in tensioning. Since the gut used for stringing is susceptible to damp, and even if kept dry loses its fine tension after awhile, attempts have been made to introduce substitutes. Wire-strung rackets were tried for a time, but the effect on the balls proved disastrous, and gut-stringing came right back into its own. The gut is treated with a preservative which helps a great deal to prolong its life.

After the racket has been strung, its handle is covered in some way, but the forms of covering are so many and various that description of them all is out of the question. The purpose, naturally, is to give a non-slipping surface for the hand of the player to grip. In some rackets, the covering is carried all the way up the handle; in others, the ends of the wood strips used for thickening the handle are visible; waxed stringing of

By courtesy of]   [A. G. Spalding & Bros. Ltd.

Threading the cross-strings.

parts of the frame is sometimes evident, and this may be to give balance by adding weight at the points where the stringing is done, or may be merely ornamental.

Now, within a limit of fourteen ounces or so, you have a very delicately-constructed tool, built up of perishable components, and subject by its stringing to a considerable strain. Quite a number of tennis players are rather careless about screwing a racket tightly into a racket-press when it is not in use, but even in a dry temperature those fine laminations of wood which compose the frame are liable to warp if left to themselves, and, though the warping may be so slight that it cannot be detected by the eye, it is enough to affect the racket and make a difference to the player. Therefore, always clamp a racket *firmly* until you want to use it again.

Water is often found in quite large natural reservoirs under the ground and here an artesian well is being drilled to reach it. Artesian wells are unusual for when the drill reaches the water, pressure forces the water up the pipe without being pumped.

COOLING WATER IN THE TROPICS.

Bottles of water, wrapped in cloth, are hung on the branches of trees and swung to and fro.

WONDERS OF OUR WATER SUPPLIES

"WATER, water everywhere, and not a drop to drink."

Has it ever occurred to you what a dreadful predicament we should be in if our water supplies became exhausted ? Water is so commonplace that we are apt to forget its importance, yet without it, of course, we could not live. Water is essential to mankind and to almost every form of life. Indeed, our very bodies are largely composed of water.

Have you ever considered the truth of the old nursery rhyme : " Little drops of water, little grains of sand, make the mighty ocean and the pleasant land."

Vapour or cloud condenses, falls to the ground in the form of rain, percolates through the earth and eventually finds its way out again in the form of springs ; these flow along as a stream to join a river, which then flows into the sea ; from the sea the water is evaporated and once more forms the clouds, only to condense again and fall as rain once more.

So the cycle goes on, and we in this country, although we sometimes grumble at the rain and the changeable climatic conditions, should really be thankful, because it is these conditions which provide us with those ample water supplies which have helped to make us the great nation that we are.

Have you ever stopped to consider where your water supply comes from ; what reserves there are and how the water is brought from the collecting ground right into your house ? In country districts water is more often than not obtained from wells, individual pumps supplying individual houses, or maybe a village pump supplies quite a number of people, or the water may come from some tiny spring which feeds a reservoir, from which it is fed to the houses. In such cases there may be a shortage of water in dry seasons unless the wells are very deep or the spring is fed from some underground natural reservoir containing a large amount of water.

In the big cities and towns, however, water is often brought very considerable distances, because the supplies from wells which originally supplied those towns years ago no longer yield sufficient for modern requirements. When this is the case, the water is brought by means of aqueducts or pipe lines. We are very proud of some of these aqueducts, as engineering feats, though really they are not to be compared with some of the aqueducts the ancient Egyptians and the Romans constructed, or the tunnels which they cut for bringing water from the mountains and hills to their centres of population. The early Greeks, too, had some wonderful examples of masonry aqueducts and tunnels. It is recorded that over six hundred years before Christ, one, Eupalinus, constructed for the water supply of Samos, a tunnel eight feet high and eight feet deep and nearly a mile long and bored through a hill, whilst in 269 B.C. the Romans are said to have completed a tunnel nearly forty-three miles long. It is also recorded that the water supply to ancient Rome was no less than one hundred million gallons daily, though this seems rather a lot, being nearly one-third as much as is used in modern London to-day : but the Romans had magnificent fountains as well as many wonderful baths. The remarkable feature of these early aqueducts and tunnels is that in those days there were no pneumatic rock drills or other scientific aids to construction such as we have to-day, and no instruments like those we have for determining levels and direction, yet these tunnels were remarkably

accurately cut.   There are still large fragments and appreciable lengths
of some of these famous aqueducts standing in Greece and Italy.

Water not only for drinking and washing, but for fountains
and swimming pools, was considered more important two or three
hundred years before Christ than it is even to-day in some country
villages in our own country !

In London, water supplies come from the Thames and from the

[*Keystone.*

A maintenance engineer testing the pumping machinery.

Lea, to supplement water which is drawn from the huge natural
underground reservoir which lies beneath London and a very wide
area of country extending all round the metropolis and beyond it.
The daily consumption of water in London alone is estimated to be
nearly four hundred million gallons in summer, of which it is estimated that forty-four million gallons come from wells of varying
depth.   Can you visualise a tank equal in area to Trafalgar Square,
London, and as high as the top of the Nelson Monument ?   Such a
tank would be emptied two and a half times daily in supplying
London's water, and the water is pumped through nearly eight

thousand miles of mains. The average water consumption of England and Wales is estimated at about 1,750,000,000 gallons per day.

Storage reservoirs ensure supplies of water after a drought of normal duration, though there have been times when the storage capacity has hardly been sufficient to outlast a long drought, and then supplies have had to be curtailed ; but there is really no need for this if sufficient reservoirs are provided, but unfortunately reservoirs are expensive things.

It was not until 1613 that London had its first reservoir, at Clerkenwell, when the population was said to go close on half a million. Now, of course, there are many reservoirs round London, and especially in the west, into which water is pumped from the Thames.

Many of our big provincial cities obtain their water from rivers also, the River Derwent supplies over eleven million gallons of

[*Will F. Taylor.*

Birmingham draws its water from this reservoir in Radnorshire. The dam is one hundred and twenty-three feet high.

Water is also used for the generation of electricity and here massive pipes are seen carrying water to turn the generators of this power station in Scotland.

water daily to Sheffield, Nottingham, Leicester, and Derby. The River Tees provides over fifteen million gallons daily to a number of towns on the north-east coast.

Birmingham, Liverpool and Manchester have gone to the hills for their water. Birmingham obtains its supplies from watersheds, or river collecting grounds near Rhyader, Radnorshire, where by damming the valleys, three huge reservoirs have been formed and two pipe lines, each seventy-five miles long, carry the water to service reservoirs on high ground surrounding the city, from whence it flows into the supply pipes or mains feeding the houses and factories.

Liverpool water travels sixty-eight miles from Lake Vyrnwy, also in North Wales, a lake which has been made, like those forming the Birmingham reservoirs, by constructing an enormous masonry dam at the end of a valley. Over fifty million gallons of water flow through the pipe lines from Vyrnwy to Liverpool every day.

Manchester obtains the bulk of its water from Thirlmere in the Lake District, no less than ninety-six miles away, but in each of these cities there are also many wells, some very deep, from which water is drawn to supply breweries, factories and other requirements.

There was a suggestion about forty-five years ago that London should augment its water supply by carrying water from the Welsh mountains, including Lake Bala, but nothing came of the scheme, which even then was estimated to cost close on twenty million pounds. This figure would probably be far exceeded to-day as will be realised when it is stated that the Liverpool Corporation Vyrnwy aqueduct cost £19,000 per mile. However, perhaps Welsh water will one day be brought to London ; either that will happen or more of the Thames winter water will have to be stored.

No water is absolutely pure, but this does not matter very much provided it does not contain injurious germs or other harmful matter. Fortunately for us our water supplies are very much purer than they are in many foreign countries, but even so, nearly all the water supplies of this country are filtered and purified before being supplied to us.

The most common method of filtration is to pass the water through huge brick chambers containing fine sand. It is rather curious that such a filter-bed not only traps dirt and impurities, it traps microbes as well, though these are trapped mainly in the fine layer or film of matter which is deposited on the top of the sand.

During the past few years additional precautions have been taken in some places, particularly where the water has been polluted in any way. The water is chlorinated. Chlorine, when added in the proportion of no more than one part to a million, kills or sterilises any microbes or germs. The chlorine is added to the water by means of special plant wherein chlorine in gaseous form is added to the water. It may be interesting to mention that water in a sunlit reservoir is said to have 98 per cent. of any bacteria or germs which it may contain removed in the course of a day or two by the action of the sun.

Water obtained from natural underground reservoirs is, in some cases, pumped into reservoirs on a hillside or on the top of a water tower, from whence it gravitates to our houses and wherever it is required. There are many types of pumps employed for this work driven by engines or electric motors, ranging from a few to hundreds of horse power, according to requirements. Some have the engines above ground, with long rods extending down the well to the pistons

A huge pumping station.

and cylinders at or below water level; others have motors above ground, driving shafts passing down the well to pumps at water level; whilst still others have both pump and motor at or even below water level. Another way of raising water is by means of compressed air; air at anything from one hundred to two or three hundred pounds pressure is led by pipes into the well and it forces the water out of the well through other pipes.

[*Alfieri.*

This water pipe is 48 inches in diameter.

In some places wells are from three hundred to four hundred feet deep, yet in others a well thirty to forty feet deep will yield as much water as those ten times as deep, according to the nature of the strata and the underground reservoirs.

To convey the water from wells to reservoirs and from reservoirs to our houses, either cast iron or steel pipes are mainly used, and nowadays these pipes are very often lined with concrete in order to prevent corrosion, for this not only reduces the size of the pipe, but it restricts the rate of flow of water in it. These pipes vary from less than an inch in diameter inside, where they come into our houses, to as much as five feet internal diameter where they lead from the reservoirs. At the reservoir end they are often controlled by valves that automatically close in the event of a burst or fractured pipe. There are also stop-cocks and control valves all along the supply line, and there should be one where the lead pipe which connects the water supply to your house enters the house; usually this is in a chamber sunk in the footpath just outside the garden gate, or if there is no garden, just alongside the house door in the footpath. Pipe and tap are usually taken two and a half to three feet below the ground so as to be below frost level.

WONDERS OF OUR WATER SUPPLIES

Passing into the house the water is taken to a tank, the supply to which is automatically controlled by a ball-tap, which is turned on by the action of a floating cylinder or ball on the end of a lever. As the water level in the tank falls, so the ball falls with it, and turns the tap on. When the water level rises again, the ball and lever rise with it and the water is turned off when the tank is full once more.

Next time you turn on the water tap, just think for a moment where the water has come from, how it has reached you, and how that which goes down the drain will eventually reach the sea, be evaporated, form clouds and in turn, rain, and perhaps come back to you again another day, just as it comes now. Though you may have plenty of water to-day, never waste it, you may be glad of it to-morrow, especially if the summer is a dry one ; besides which, every drop of water brought through an aqueduct or pipe line, or drawn from a well, creates wear, which though infinitesimal will have to be paid for by someone some day ; and above all be thankful you live in a country where there are, as a rule, ample supplies of pure, fresh water.

[*Photopress.*

Air under pressure is blown through a rapid filter to remove clogging materials.

MAKING AN ELECTRIC LAMP

THE first electric lamps were made by hand. They were very expensive, and had only a very short life. The life of an electric lamp is the period for which it continues to give a good light. Nowadays, the average life of a lamp of a good make is taken to be one thousand hours, and in spite of the fact that electric lamps to-day are mass-produced, almost entirely by machinery, they are far more efficient and of course, far cheaper, than they were when laboriously hand made.

An electric lamp consists of several parts. There is the glass bulb, the glass rod which carries the wires, the support wires, the filament and the cap with which the bulb is closed to make the necessary contacts. The raw materials in the lamp socket are of considerable importance. Different kinds of glass are used for the bulb and for the rod. In making the bulb a crown or soda glass is employed, because this is most easily worked by machinery. For the rod, which has to be subjected to considerable heat inside the bulb, a lead glass is used, and its composition has to be very carefully maintained, for it must expand under heat as nearly as possible at the same rate and to the same amount as the wires which it contains. If there were any great differ-

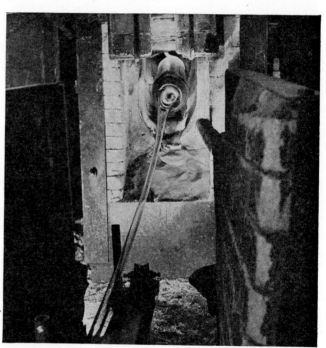

By courtesy of]   [The General Electric Co., Ltd.

AN AUTOMATIC TUBE-DRAWING MACHINE (FURNACE END).

The lead glass used for the tubing flows from the fireclay crucible containing the molten glass, or " metal " as it is called, on to a rotating cylindrical fireclay mandril, and at the same time, a jet of air is forced down the centre of the mandril. The massive tube thus formed is drawn off continuously down a runway of about one hundred and sixty feet, at the end of which it is cut off in four-foot lengths. These are automatically gauged for diameter, and the ends glazed by gas jets.

ence in the rate of expansion of the glass and wire when heated, the vacuum inside would not be maintained.

Three different kinds of wires may be fitted to an electric lamp. The wires which travel down the glass rod carrying the current are generally of a special nickel-iron alloy, while the filament itself is usually of tungsten. The metal tungsten has been found satisfac-

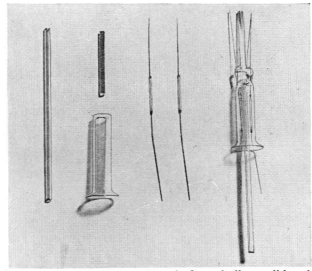

Hollow tube for exhausting air from bulb ; solid rod support for filament (*above*) and flange (*below*) ; lead-in wires ; completion of " pinch ", sealing in the rod, lead-in wires and exhaust tube inside the flange.

tory for filament wires because it emits an intense light at comparatively low temperature, well below its melting point, and because it disintegrates slowly when heated to a very high temperature. In the history of the electric lamp, many other substances have been used for filaments, beginning with carbon, which had the disadvantage of giving a comparatively poor light at the low temperatures to which heating it

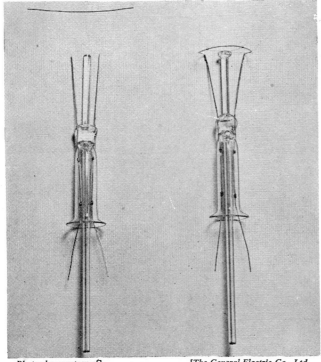

Photos by courtesy of] [The General Electric Co., Ltd.
(*Left*) Filament ready for connection to lead-in wires.
(*Right*) Filament in position, with its supports.

was safe. The carbon did not melt, but easily disintegrated during service. Carbon filaments are still used for some lamps, more especially those which have to be handled rather roughly. The support wires are commonly constructed of molybdenum, another comparatively rare metal, which is used in preference to tungsten for support wires because it is so much stronger.

These are the raw materials of the electric lamps which light our homes. The first step in manufacture is to prepare the wire.

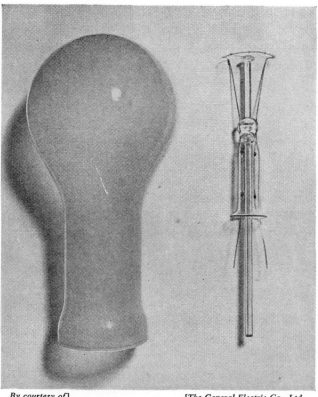

Bulb ready to receive filament assembly. Note " neck " at bottom of bulb, which is cut off when the bulb and flange are sealed together.

Every lamp manufacturer has his secrets, but the general principles are now fairly well known. When tungsten was first used, the powdered oxide was mixed with a binding material and squirted through a die, the fine wire thus obtained being " burnt off " to get rid of the binding material. To-day the fine metallic powder is pressed by heavy hydraulic rams into blocks about twelve inches long. These blocks are then placed under mechanical hammers which beat them until a long rod is formed. This is heated to about one thousand degrees Centigrade and squeezed through a die, the resulting wire being between one-hundredth and one-fifteenth of a millimetre in diameter. The actual diameter depends upon the power of the finished lamp.

Meanwhile the glass bulb has been prepared, and the blowing of these bulbs for lamps is entirely automatic. The arm of an automatic machine descends into a tank of molten glass, picks up just the required quantity of glass as a knob and deposits it in a mould, where it is blown into the desired shape. The trimming of the surplus glass off the bulb is also carried out automatically. The glass tubing is prepared by another automatic machine and the requisite length of wire drawn through it.

Perhaps the most important stage in the manufacture of an electric lamp is the exhaustion of the bulb. If a lamp were filled with air, it would be very quickly burnt out, owing to the inter-action of the metallic filament, when heated, with the oxygen and moisture in the air. The bulbs are, therefore, almost completely exhausted of air by pumps. This stage of the manufacture is also automatic, the bulbs being placed on a rotating turntable to which they may be fed by hand. In actual practice it is impossible for the bulbs to be completely exhausted by the pumps, and further treatment is necessary to ensure that no oxygen or water-vapour is left inside.

The treatment varies in the case of the vacuum lamp or the gas-filled lamp. In the vacuum lamp, a process called "cleaning up" is carried out. This merely consists of placing inside the lamp a very small quantity of a phosphorus compound. After the lamp has been closed, an electric current is passed through it, the

By courtesy of]   [The General Electric Co., Ltd.

(*Left*) After sealing in, the bulb is ready to receive the cap.
(*Right*) The completed lamp.

phosphorus compound taking out the surplus oxygen which may have been absorbed, or " occluded," by the glass. In the manu-facture of gas-filled lamps, the inside is " washed out " as it were, with nitrogen, which is an inert gas. In either event, great care is taken to see that no trace of oxygen or moisture is left inside.

While these operations have been going on, other machines have

By courtesy of]   [The General Electric Co., Ltd.

AN AUTOMATIC BULB-BLOWING MACHINE.
In the top right corner the suction arms are withdrawing glass from the furnace. Round the lower circumference of the machine is a series of moulds open to receive the molten glass.

been stamping out caps from sheets of brass. The glass rod and filament are attached and the case is sealed into place. The lamp is now ready, except for the final process of having the maker's name, the voltage and the wattage, etched on the surface with hydrofluoric acid. " Frosting " is carried out in the same way. There follows a final trial in which the lamps are tested for the amount of light they give, and for their consumption of current. In the testing process, automatic machinery is also used, the lamps

The finest sizes of wire are drawn on these small machines.   A single Tungsten bar
yields up to 30 miles of these wires.

Photos by courtesy of]   [*The General Electric Co., Ltd.*

This machine cements the cap to the lamp and solders the lead-in wires to the cap-
contacts.

on a turn-table coming one after the other to the contacts of the try-out circuit or switch.

A very high standard is set to-day, and a lamp is supposed to last for at least one thousand hours at ninety per cent. efficiency. In most cases the difference between a good electric light and one of poor characteristics, is not the intensity of light that is given, or even perhaps the length of its life, but the amount of current consumed. Even now most of the energy of an electric-light filament is dissipated as heat and only about two-and-a-half per cent. of the energy is actually turned into light. There is room for improvement.

[The General Electric Co., Ltd.

MAKING FLUORESCENT LAMPS.
The tubes on the right have been emptied, leaving a thin fluorescent coating inside.